Ron Arad

Shin and Tomoko Azumi

Rowan and Erwan Bouroullec

Matali Crasset

Nick Crosbie

DUMoffice

Mark Dytham/KDa

Martí Guixé

Thomas Heatherwick

Scott Henderson

Ichiro Iwasaki

Hella Jongerius

RADI Designers

Karim Rashid

Tejo Remy

Arnout Visser

Marcel Wanders

Tokujin Yoshioka

Inspir-ing

a sourcebook

Black Dog Publishing

design-ers

Paul Rodgers

contents

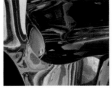
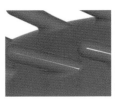

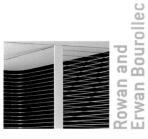

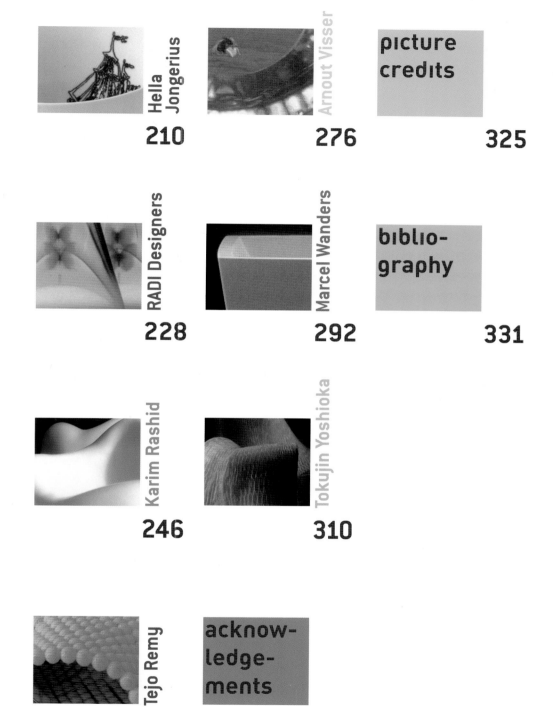

The importance of inspiration sources and the way designers use them, particularly in the early stages of the design process, is widely acknowledged and well documented.[1] The origin of design ideas or inspiration behind some of the fantastic design concepts we witness has been the focus of recent investigation. In a recent article in the Italian design magazine *Domus*, a selection of seven internationally acclaimed designers including Ross Lovegrove and Marc Newson were interviewed and asked what inspired and informed their design work.[2] The responses from the designers involved in the study came from widely diverse fields including architecture, cinema, solar cars, biomorphic technology and space exploration projects.

Designers are driven by profoundly different influences and issues. The great Italian designer Alessandro Mendini is quoted as being inspired by the paintings of de Chirico, whereas Gaetano Pesce is motivated by empty bottles — beer, mineral water, and even black wine bottles. Ingo Maurer states that mono-racial societies make him feel claustrophobic.[3] Such are the preferences and prejudices that make up the modern face of design.

Designers find inspiration in many things, from both the natural and artificial world. They are influenced in their conscious and subconscious perceptions of the world.[4] In many design disciplines, including architecture, product design, fashion design, and graphic design, it is commonplace for both 'iconic' and 'canonic' inspiration sources to be used and applied in new projects.[5] Iconic inspiration sources tend to come from objects, such as products, buildings, and cars, that are ordinarily found in the modern (artificial) world, but also from fields outside design.[6] One well known example of iconic inspiration from the natural world is the adoption of the burdock plant's 'fruit', which are covered with sharp hooks. This is generally accepted as the major source of inspiration in the development of VELCRO in the early 1940s.[7] Canonic inspiration sources are based on abstract geometrical patterns, such as proportional grids. Examples of this type of inspiration include the "golden section" and Le Corbusier's "Le Modulor" measurement system.[8] This book focuses on how 18 of the world's leading designers are motivated by 'iconic' forms of inspiration in their work.

More recently other iconic inspiration examples, from an architectural design context, include the work of Frank Gehry and Future Systems. Both of these practices have received widespread recognition for their creative use of design inspiration sources. Gehry, responsible for the design of the hugely successful Guggenheim Museum in Bilbao, lists one of his main sources of design inspiration as "fish".

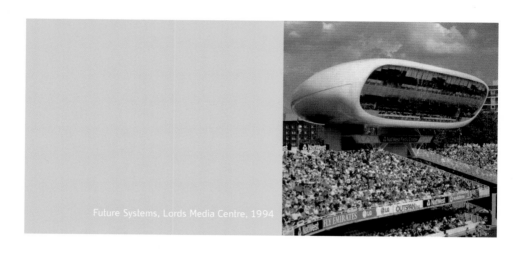

Future Systems, Lords Media Centre, 1994

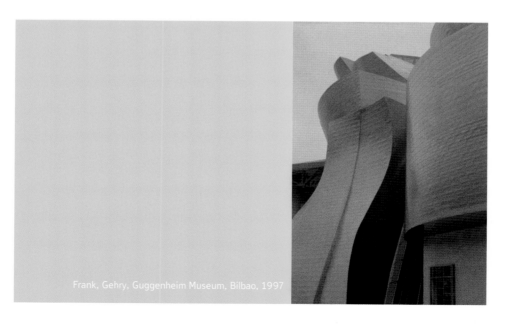

Frank, Gehry, Guggenheim Museum, Bilbao, 1997

Future Systems, on the other hand, are well known for their extraordinary range of inspiration sources in their work, such as the use of cross-sectional views of racing yachts in the design of the Lords Media Centre, London.[9]

In the domain of product design, inspiration sources are also viewed as a significant factor in the development of successful, unique and innovative objects. Philippe Starck, whose work ranges from chic hotels to chairs to lamps to toothbrushes, and is considered by many to be the most famous designer in the world at present, lists several culturally significant icons from film, music, art, design, and nature as inspirational in his work. Starck in the frontispiece of his book mentions his heroes from the past and present, day as Alexander Calder, Erich Mendelsohn, Jean-Luc Godard, Shiro Kuramata, and the frozen sea, to name but a few.[10]

Moreover, in the field of furniture design, the hugely successful Michael Young includes the work of the American conceptual artist Jeff Koons, old tractors and milk bottles in his list of wide ranging inspiration sources.[11] Similarly, the British furniture designer Matthew Hilton has used imagery and inspiration sources in his 'Wait' plastic chair from classic furniture icons of the 1960s and 70s including Vico Magistretti's Selene chair and Joe Colombo's Universale chair.[12] The significance and use of iconic inspiration sources in design is, thus, not in question. Indeed, it is widely recognised and reported that inspiration sources play a key role in the development of successful products.

This book reveals what motivates and influences some of the world's most successful designers in the creation of their outstanding work. The designers have been drawn from a number of current design centres throughout the world (i.e. New York, London, Paris, Amsterdam, Rotterdam, Tokyo, Barcelona) and chosen on their current contribution to contemporary design practice and thinking. Each designer was interviewed in their own studio using a qualitative interview technique, which allows for a range of topics to be covered in an informal manner.[13] Each interview set out to explore the range of cultural influences from the worlds of art, design, film, literature, architecture, car design, music, media and inspirational people of each designer. The nature of each interview meant that the designers were relaxed, comfortable and free to outline, often in great detail, the extent of their personal cultural influences. The interviews obviously differ significantly from one designer to the next, but they each provide a rare and valuable insight into the minds of the designers involved.

The book, therefore, helps us as observers map and connect the significant personal network of influences and range of cultural icons the designers use. Each interview is presented here as it actually happened, and while some editing has been necessary the coloquial language and tone of each designers' 'voice' has been left more-or-less as is. It is thereby hoped that the reader of this book will get an idea of where each of the 18 designers are going in their work, where they are coming from, what influences they share with other designers, and which influences are unique to them, as well as something of their humour and, often, lateral creative thinking.

NOTES

1 Heylighen, A, and Verstijnen, IM, "Exposure to Examples: Exploring CBD in Architectural Education", in JS Gero, ed, *Artificial Intelligence in Design 2000*, The Netherlands: Kluwer Academic 2000, pp. 413-432; Oxman, RE, "Prior Knowledge in Design: A Dynamic Knowledge-based Model of Design and Creativity", *Design Studies*, 11(1), 1990, pp. 17-28.

2 Capella, J, Masceroni, L and Picchi, F, "The Roots of Design", *Domus*, 812, 1999, pp. 59-73; Rawsthorn, A, *Marc Newson*, London: Booth-Clibborn Editions, 1999.

3 Busch, A, ed, *Design is Words, Things, People, Buildings and Places*, New York: Metropolis Books and Princeton Architectural Press, 2002.

4 Vrontikis, P, *Inspiration=Ideas: A Creativity Source book for Graphic Designers*, Gloucester, Massachusetts: Rockport Publishers Inc, 2002.

5 Heylighen, A, *In Case of Architectural Design: Critique and Praise of Case-Based Design in Architecture*, PhD Thesis, Belgium: Katholieke Universiteit Leuven, 2000.

6 Petroski, H, *The Evolution of Useful Things*, New York: Vintage Books, 1994.

7 Wake, WK and Kornhaber, ML, *Design Paradigms: A Sourcebook for Creative Visualization*, New York: John Wiley and Sons, 2000.

8 Broadbent, G, *Design in Architecture: Architecture and the Human Sciences*, London: John Wiley and Sons, 1973.

9 Future Systems, *More for Inspiration Only*, London: Academy Editions, 1999.

10 Starck, P, ed, *Starck*, Cologne: Taschen, 2000.

11 Payne, A, *We Like This!*, London: Black Dog Publishing, 1999.

12 McDermott, C, and Dewing, D, *Matthew Hilton: Furniture for Our Time*, London: Lund Humphries/Ashgate Publishing Limited, 2000.

13 Mason, J, *Qualitative Researching*, London: Sage, 1996; Rubin, HJ and Rubin, IS, *Qualitative Interviewing: The Art of Hearing Data*, London: Sage, 1995.

All other images featured in the book are courtesy Black Dog Publishing or Paul Rogers.
Those images not identified by a designers name are the work of the designer featured in each of the book's sections.

Ron Arad

Ron Arad initially studied at the Jerusalem Academy of Art, but moved to London, in 1974, and studies at the Architectural Association. In 1981 he established One Off — a design studio, workshop and showroom in Covent Garden. He founded Ron Arad Associates in 1989 — an architecture and design practice based in London, and with design and production unit in Como, Italy.

Ron Arad's studio is increasingly known for the production of individual pieces made of sheet steel or plastic, which always mischievously exploit their formal and functional possibilities to the fullest. The sculptural forms often have an unexpected impact which first emerges during use. At the same time these works are just as much the result of the experimental attitude that goes on in his workshop.

Arad is currently Professor of Design Products at the Royal College of Art, London. In 1994 Ron Arad was made Guest Editor of the *International Design Yearbook* and in 2002 he was the Chief Editor of the *Product Design Review Book*. He is the recipient of numerous design and production awards.

Big Easy Chair, 1988

I come from a fine art background, but somehow I found myself studying architecture at the Architectural Association (AA), London. At that time the AA seemed to be more of an 'art school' than an art school itself. It was a really exciting time, as no one seemed to actually be building anything. The AA was full of all sorts of things, from films to performances. It was full of experiments. There were all sorts of things going on, using spaces, substances and I don't know what. It looked to me like a 'motorcycle place', a 'sex place'... so I joined the queue and they interviewed me. Basically they asked me, "Why do you want to be an architect?" I replied that my mother wanted me to be an architect. I told them she was an artist and for some reason they offered me a place and I took it. I believe I was always an outsider to my studies. I was more into studying Marcel Duchamp than Marcel Breuer.

For me there has never been anything or anybody as influential as Duchamp. Absolutely never! When you are making a name for yourself in design and people start interviewing you, and asking you about influences, you have to find some answers. So, there is, of course, Jean Prouvé and Achille Castiglioni, and later Gaetano Pesce, but they are not of the same calibre as Duchamp. I would say the reason I have mentioned these three designers is that at some time they have all challenged conventional thinking about design. Pesce to this day still thinks he is Picasso.

I don't have a lot of rules that I care enough about to break. But I have, somehow, been born into this profession. Why I do not know. It does not come with anger. I was, if you like, very spoilt and privileged from an early age. Maybe I had no one to play cards with, or maybe no one understood me, or perhaps my parents didn't understand me. I don't know, I have very little to complain about, except that I grew up in the Middle East with wars all around me, and all that. I was not alone with it. I prefer a global culture.
In the 1960s it was good. It was very good. It was a very interesting time. We were all very optimistic about things. We all thought we were going to change the world very soon, and that the rest would be left behind in their pink stripy ties.

In terms of contemporaries, I have a lot of time for Thomas Heatherwick. I love his work. I like the way he is very inventive in his work. I mean, he is not part of any trend. You know, he is just slowly promising to deliver, to explore things. His work is always interesting, and it's not just another stylised chair. I like that. I wanted him to teach at the Royal College of Art (RCA), but he is still shying away from me at the moment. I would love him to teach, but he says not yet.

Ron Arad

I have also been trying to get Thomas to design products. I think, with most of his work being large-scale installations or spaces, he definitely has products in him. I don't know if he showed you the bags that he has designed with zips. Fantastic stuff, very exciting. I think he is for real. Thomas Heatherwick is definitely for real.

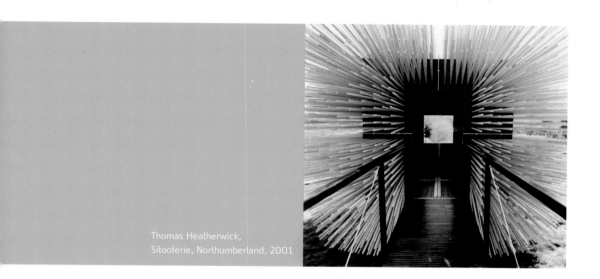

Thomas Heatherwick,
Sitooterie, Northumberland, 2001

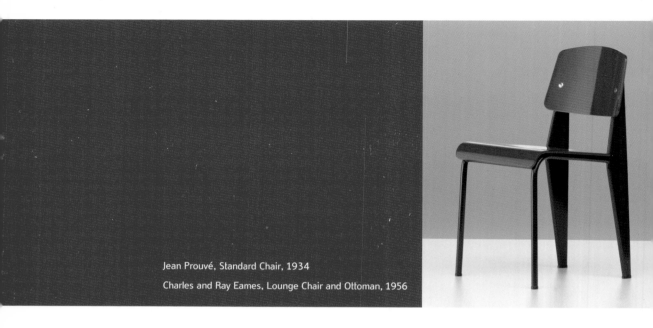

Jean Prouvé, Standard Chair, 1934

Charles and Ray Eames, Lounge Chair and Ottoman, 1956

Ron Arad

The Rover Chair, 1981

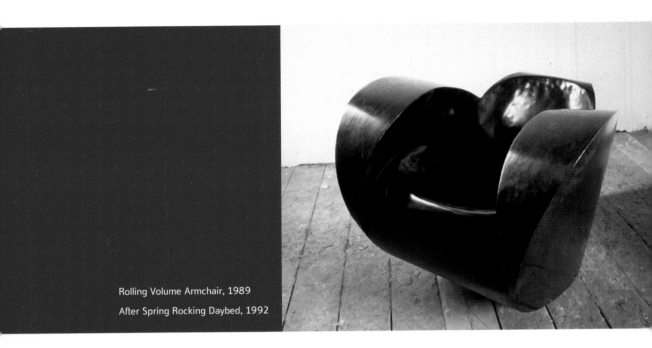

Rolling Volume Armchair, 1989

After Spring Rocking Daybed, 1992

Ron Arad

Bookworm Shelving System, 1994

Ron Arad 17

Of course, if you had to name one building, it would have to be Le Corbusier's Ronchamp. For many, many years, pictures and drawings existed of Ronchamp, yet no one went to see it. But then there is also the Berlin Philharmonic. I think Frank Gehry, in general, gets away with things that other people don't. For any other architect, doing sculptural work is taboo, but Gehry does it. Gehry does it extraordinarily well. I admire Gehry for some of his projects, absolutely. If you follow his career through the years, he hasn't changed his style or approach to suit anyone. Some of his buildings are certainly more striking than others, particularly those of the 'early years' which is maybe because there were not so many of them. The best measure when you look at architecture is if it makes you jealous. I do get jealous of Gehry's work. And I have been jealous of Nouvel's work. I mean I have a lot of time for Jean Nouvel. He is, again, fantastic. He possesses a strong independence in what he does, and he does it within the very thick of the profession. And the profession is not a very nice profession — the architecture profession. It is sort of like oral sex. I don't really have the confidence to be ticking over, churning out some horrible project. I say horrible because of the clients, the brief and the strangeness. Nouvel has done well because he operates from the middle of the profession, and I admire that.

Ron Arad

Le Corbusier, Notre Dame du Haut, Ronchamp, France, 1950–1955

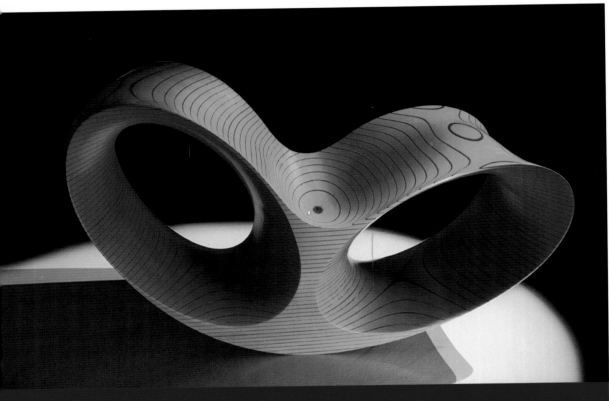

Oh Void, 2004

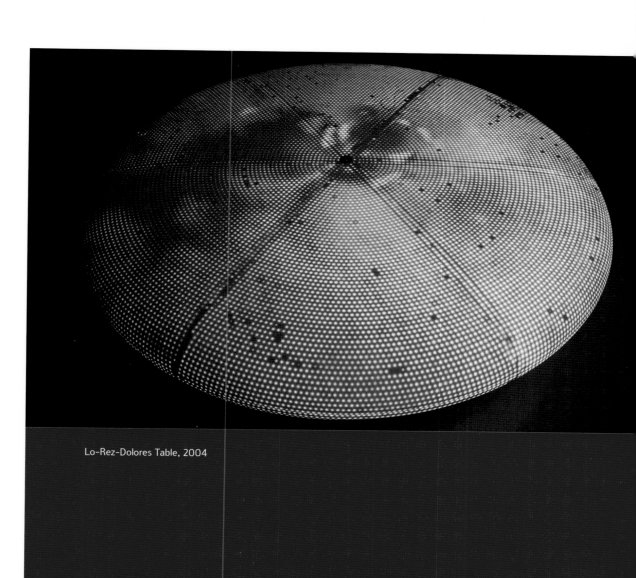

Lo–Rez–Dolores Table, 2004

You know about my aversion to the arrogance in design. I do believe that what we do here in this studio is largely more interesting than what most other designers have been doing. And I have not make a lot of effort to make this visible to other people. Some of it just comes across. I think I am very nice to people — to anyone who comes to the studio here. I will not be snotty with them. I will give them time. Is this arrogant? I don't know. I do believe what we do is best — but it is.

I turn down quite a lot of work because some of it does not make sense. I would not work on something like the re-design of an ashtray for example. What have I turned down? I was asked to design a sex aid — a vibrator, which I have absolutely nothing against. But they wanted to have a Ron Arad vibrator and I did not like that idea at all. Apparently, there will be Mark Newson and Tom Dixon vibrators available very soon. They obviously felt differently to me.

Perhaps my honeymoon period is over at the RCA. But I have to say that the students who design products at the RCA leave very, very confident and they believe fully in everything they do. They think what they think matters, and that is good. Maybe there should be a better word than arrogance.

There are tonnes of products that I think are fantastic. Simple things, like Arne Jacobsen's Ant Chair which sold over eight million copies, and Denmark has about six million people. So, there is a chair out there for every Dane, and then some. And no one can design a chair much better than that. This is good, because that is what we are trying to do here. Of course, I have to mention Charles and Ray Eames, and George Nelson, obviously.

The Human Stain by Philip Roth, it's an amazing book. I will spoil it for you — it's about a black man, a professor who at some point in his life registers as white because his physical appearance allows him to. The first half of the book is spent 'revealing' him. It's a wonderful book. I also like William Gibson's work. I don't like science fiction that much, but what is amazing about Gibson is that he really knows about it and can describe it. He can describe things — the processes, real science fiction, not the stuff about 100 years from now, but better. Read Gibson. Read *All Tomorrow's Parties*, it's very good.

I fly a lot and I don't like films on aeroplanes, so I read a lot. I also think there are many events forcing us to watch the news on TV these days. The things there are many happening in the world now, more than before, mean that we need to keep ourselves informed. I happened to be in New York on September 11, so I am, more than ever, keen to know what is happening. So, I am afraid, *Newsnight* takes up some valuable reading time.

Philip Roth,
The Human Stain,
book jacket, 2000

William Gibson,
All Tomorrow's Parties,
book jacket, 1999

The Citröen DS is without competition.
A great car, totally new from an
automotive design perspective.

Citroën DS, c. 1967

cars

The Citroën DS is without competition. A great car, totally new from an
automotive design perspective. For the last 20 years I have driven an old
Fiat 500. It refuses to die and it glows in the dark. My students at the
RCA painted it a glow-in-the-dark colour.

I think films can be hugely influential, especially when they are relevant to what we do here. I would say Jacques Tati and films like *Playtime* and *Traffic*, in particular. The thing is, Godard was very influential, but I don't know if I would enjoy his films as much now as I used to. I came to London probably because I had this stilted image from films. There is the David Mercer film, *A Suitable Case For Freedom*, but, of course, I didn't find the period of 'grey realism'. When I came here it did not wait for me. That world could not live forever.

I still go to the cinema, usually in Leicester Square. I would say that 80 per cent of the cinema audience there are movie addicts. And the cinema is for under 18s, which means most of the time I am sick of cinemas. But when I am on an aeroplane to Tokyo, for example, I can choose from 16 films and usually I can hardly find a film I would like to watch. With the big films I don't feel I'm missing anything, but when there is a good film it's fantastic. I mean, the worst film ever is *Moulin Rouge*. I had the pleasure of going to the opening night. I could not decide which was worse, the party or the film. The film probably takes the biscuit. It's a disgusting film. It is probably enough for you to know that there is a guy called Toulouse Lautrec in the film. The only connection he had to Toulouse Lautrec was that he was an oaf. The film does not mention the fact that he was a painter, a genius. There was nothing French about the film, and ugly acting — what a waste!

Godard was very influential, but I don't know if I would enjoy his films as much as I used to.

Jean-Luc Godard, À bout de souffle, promotional postcard, 1960

As I mentioned earlier, I come from a fine art background, but somehow found myself studying architecture. This was during the 1960s when London was full of experimentation — all sorts of things. I think I was always a bit of an outsider when I was studying architecture. I really admired Duchamp because of his defiance of the mainstream and his aversion to conformity. He invented his own rules, and he continually questioned authority and art history. He would make an ironing board out of a Rembrandt painting, or a piece of card, or a discarded bottle. At the same time I like difference. I mean, my skill had to do with pencils and drawings. I come from being in a group that is contextually known as "good at art" at school. At an early age if I did a portrait that had a good likeness, people would want to keep it, but I wouldn't be satisfied with it. It was not this or that model — you have cameras, so who cares about drawing? So, I had this attraction to pencils, and I would say that there is much more to drawing... perhaps this is why I ended up as a designer. In terms of artists who have influenced me, there have been millions of them. I like Pop Art in general, especially Jasper Johns and Claus Oldenburg. I can draw stubs of cigarettes very, very artistically. Shapes, sometimes I sort of like android things, you know. It's only later that I discovered the field of design and found myself there. Being a designer was not really in the cards at all. For me, however, there has never been anything or anybody as influential as Marcel Duchamp. Never!

Music does inspire me. I mean, tons, such as Lou Reed, The Velvet Underground, and David Byrne — they are all favourites of mine. And then there is Bob Dylan. There was a time when I wanted to be Dylan much more than Duchamp, but I don't think there was room for two Bob Dylans in this world. I admire Bob Dylan because he continues to break his own rules, and in doing this creates certain expectations, and then he just goes and breaks these rules again somewhere else. He upsets lots of people. Why does he do this? Don't ask me! Ask a whole generation why, they know. I was surprised when I went to a Bob Dylan concert and there were more than 60,000 people there. I don't think from the stage that you could single him out as the best, he is just one. So, there is pop music, underground music. I also listen to Schubert, Bartok, Stravinsky, and a lot of Cuban music.

David Byrne,
Look into the Eyeball, CD cover, 2001

Lou Reed,
Rock n Roll Animal, CD cover, 1966

I read *The Guardian* every morning. I also read the *Independent on Sunday*, and *The Observer*. I don't read weeklies that much. And I looked at *Hello* and *OK!* in the waiting room of my doctor's surgery the other day. Excellent!

people

I think the greatest politician in my lifetime was Anwar Sadat. He came to the political arena out of the blue. He flew from Cairo to Tel Aviv, risking his life in a way, and gave his life in the hope of stopping bloodshed and war. Of course, this didn't work, but it took a great, great man to do such a thing and I wish there were someone like him around now. Today, most politicians are pathetic, no one comes close to Sadat. In the Middle East today, most of the people are just wolves, mumbling the right things, but still making no progress towards peace.

I mean, you sometimes hear a snippet or two from a politician and think that he or she has got something to say. You identify with them and think she or he might be a winner and not a loser — someone like Claire Short, the way her idealistic youth has given way to statesmanship. I don't mind this. But what is awful is someone like Jack Straw. Mo Mowlam, however, is someone that I feel has admirable qualities. I am not interested in middle ground politics. I used to hate Giuliani because we were always told he was a great guy, he wrote this, and he did this and that. But on television, when I was in New York on September 11, he was a giant. He was a big contrast to George W Bush. There was, you could see, a man, a real person in Giuliani. And maybe, up there, he rose to a tragedy. A horrible tragedy. But why ask me? I am only a designer, not a politician.

If I were to host a dinner party, I think I would invite honest, generous people. I am telling you this on a personal level. When I was in Tokyo, I met Issey Miyake and he is truly a really great person. I have never seen such generosity in one individual. I went to Tokyo with some of my students, and Miyake made us very welcome. It was not a delegated generosity. It was for real, and it was very personal. Plus he is a giant in everything that he does in terms of design. He is a true survivor. He is a great, great man. And occasionally when we meet people who are absolutely gifted at what they do and who are prominent in their profession, you know why they are so important. Individuals such as Terry Jones. To have dinner with him would be memorable. You know why he is amazing? It is because his humour is still alive and fresh today. I think he is the most creative of the Monty Python team. If I were to give you other examples, it would turn into a name dropping session.

Ron Arad

Anwar Sadat
Claire Short
Terry Jones
Mo Mowlan

Shin and Tomoko Azumi

Shin and Tomoko Azumi were both born in Japan — Shin in Kobe in 1965 and Tomoko in Hiroshima in 1966. They met at the Kyoto City University of Art where they studied Product Design and environmental design, respectively. In 1992 Shin commenced his studies in Industrial Design at the Royal College of Art, London, with Tomoko moving to London with him to start the RCA's Furniture Design Course in 1993.

Shin and Tomoko Azumi established the AZUMI Design Studio, London, in 1995. Since then the Studio has been exploring new areas of design across product, furniture, space and technology related environments. The Azumis started to establish themselves by putting limited editions into production and gradually winning commercial commissions. They concentrated on pieces which could be economically produced in small quantities, such as the apparently simple, but conceptually ingenuous wooden Table=Chest and Wire Frame chairs and benches made from ready-made industrial material inspired by supermarket baskets.

Since the inception of AZUMI Design Studio their work has featured in a number of public collections, including the Victoria and Albert Museum, the Crafts Council and the Geffrye Museum. The Azumis also possess an impressive international client list in areas including product, furniture and spatial design, such as Authentics, Guzzini and Habitat.

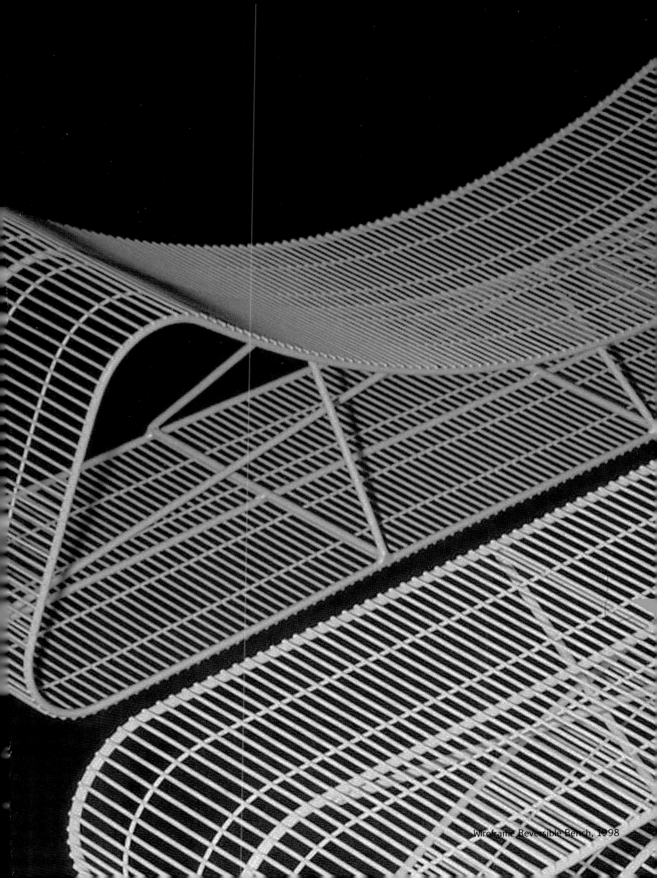

Wireframe Reversible Bench, 1998

Shin: For me, Castiglioni is the person who I really admire the most.

Tomoko: Vico Magistretti for me.

Shin: Not Buckminster Fuller for you?

Tomoko: Yes, Buckminster Fuller maybe. But, he's not really a designer. He's more a philosopher.

Shin: So many people, actually, all in there. If we start thinking about kinds of influences, everything is an influence and I cannot list everything, but the strongest influence is probably Castiglioni. In particular, Castiglioni's diversity of viewpoints on design. He has danced in an interesting way. You know, his design approach is not one direction. He has got diversity within his own approach. This is a point that I really appreciate. His designs are more about ideas rather than...

Tomoko: ... shape.

Shin: Shape is coming really naturally from his innovative ideas. That is a point which we really admire. One of the most important things in our design work is the idea. It could be a very practical idea or it could be quite a poetic idea, but the idea part is the most important part. And the shape of the design, the form of the design follows naturally, purely follows from that idea. So, we really appreciate the attitude of Castiglioni and his driving towards a very universal way of looking at things.

Tomoko: Observing daily life, I think, he picks up small hints of daily life and then expands these into design.

Shin: Our interests are about interactivity and movement. We love the theatre very much and it is one of our main sources of ideas. Our favourite theatre director is a Canadian, Robert Lepage. He did several performances at the Edinburgh Festival. He did *Midsummer Night's Dream* in 1992, and *Geometry of Miracles* at the National Theatre, which is about Frank Lloyd Wright and Russian Constructivism. His visual effects are amazing. Everything is on one stage, so many ideas to amuse people.

Tomoko: Sometimes he uses water, shadows, and light.

Shin: Materials, visuals and gravity. Also, he uses the whole space of the theatre as the stage, not only the ground, but above, too. He uses the whole space and creates an illusion of anti-gravity. For example, in *Midsummer Night's Dream*, he used a contortionist as the character Puck. Using the contortionist, he created an illusion of something very immediate, with flexible, strange shapes and movement. The character Puck speaks very fluently and he is not only on the ground but also in the air, using ropes. This is pretty amazing on stage. How Lepage surprises people, the quantity and quality of ideas, and how he makes people enjoy themselves is amazing.

Tomoko: It is very interesting to collaborate with dancers and performers.

Shin: For us as designers, what we are doing almost every time is creating an 'introduction' using a living body. The topic is about life, atmosphere, and activity.

Tomoko: Or relationships between the human being and the object.

Shin: We try not to present an object as it is. We always think about the object within the context of the introduction to the people. That is the thing we are influenced by, and which we have done.

Everything is an influence and I cannot list everything, but the strongest influence is probably Castiglioni. In particular, Castiglioni's diversity of viewpoints on design. He has danced around in an interesting way.

Achille and Pier Giacomo Castiglioni, Sella Stool, 1957

Shin and Tomoko Azumi

Le Corbusier, Villa Savoye,
Poissy-sur-Seine, 1929-1930

Shin: I've never had any architectural experience that has deeply influenced me. Maybe, Expo 70 in Osaka.

Tomoko: Do you remember who planned that architecture?

Shin: I don't know. Lots and lots of different architects designed the individual pavilions. When I was five years old, I was brought to the Expo 70 festival. I was really shocked by the sense of this future vision. They presented this vision where everything was so futuristic, and it was very exciting. Maybe this is not a direct influence on our work.

Shin: Apart from that, I appreciate quite a lot of architects' work. Le Corbusier, of course, I really appreciate. I was so amazed by his architecture. Ronchamp is very interesting.

Tomoko: Personally, I like the private house near Paris by Le Corbusier. I personally like that, its use of space, and how you take the person from the entrance to the living area and that sort of planning.

Shin: Tomoko is more from an architectural background. I'm more, in a sense, the person who is looking at the object.

Tomoko: I remember Noguchi's bridge in Hiroshima, in front of the Peace Park, which marks the centre of the atomic bomb blast. I remember that very organic, very symbolic bridge, which I saw a lot in my childhood. And when I saw the exhibition of Noguchi at the Design Museum, I thought, "yeah, that gave me something in my childhood". It was quite significant.

Shin and Tomoko Azumi

Shin: In terms of innovation in the world, which really opened up my mind, the greatest personal experience I've ever had with an object is with the saxophone. I play the saxophone. This real, basic experience is completely different to what I'm used to when designing, because this object is designed purely for sound. It is a very uncomfortable instrument to play. And it requires so much effort for me to play, it needs a lot of practice, and it has a very complicated interface. I started having a really creative feeling of attachment, physically and mentally, to this object. This direct connection, from the soul to the sound. I feel the instrument is part of my body, which is quite an unusual experience. So, this is a really significant object for me personally. I don't know if it could be said for the general public, but it is my personal feeling for the object.

The other thing that positively shocked me was the Walkman. That was another good shock. When I started using the Walkman I was an older teenager, middle to old teenager, very sentimentally minded. I'd listen to music outside and the scenery would look completely different with the view and the background music, and I felt like I was part of a movie or something. The effect of scenery and listening to the music in a casual way was sometimes fantastic. I was so surprised and I was mentally affected by that positive change. The Walkman was for me a fantastic combination of watching things with music.

Tomoko: You choose your own music.

Shin: The Walkman was a great experience that is typical of technological equipment.

Tomoko: I think I'm influenced by the daily object that I've used from my childhood, which is chopsticks. These are functional objects which you can use to cut, you can scoop, you can stick, you can move from the bowl to the mouth, or you can do very small things with two chopsticks. When we design something and wish to have one object with more than one function, we always think about what chopsticks can do, and what the object can do in more than one way. So, chopsticks are a banal object that we use and like, and they make something simple like eating a beautiful experience.

Shin and Tomoko Azumi

Tomoko: A book by Bernard Rudofsky, *Architecture Without Architects* has influenced me a lot. He picked up lots of banal architecture. Like in the middle of China where they dig up the land, and make houses under the land or very light structured houses that you can carry somewhere, in Papua New Guinea. He had an exhibition in New York in the 1950s and he collected all these things and claimed that not only architects can create the real thing. *In Praise of Shadow* is another one. It's by Tanizaki. He's a novelist but this is a statement.

Shin: It's the post war period, just after World War Two. He is writing about the beauty of the traditional living environment. He is warning about what we get with convenient materials and what we loose from the way of life in the past. He was trying to analyse precisely what life was like in the past and how we have to be cautious in the future.

Tomoko: At that moment in Japan, people started to introduce a lot of electrical things in houses and that started to ruin traditional lives, so the book was about warning how beautiful the traditional life was. Because we work after the introduction of these electrical things, it was very refreshing to read this book. And we then started to learn what we could do without modern equipment and things like that.

Shin: In terms of a novelist, I'm very influenced by a Japanese poet, Shuntaro Tanikawa. He translates things like Snoopy and Mother Goose into Japanese. I follow his writings. His explanation is very precise, like a haiku. It is trying to be everything, very ambitious, four or five meanings within one word. Within the lines, 7-5-7, a poet tries to contain so much meaning, as well as the superficial. There are several layers of meaning. Sometimes it makes the work very ambitious. What Tanikawa did, was he followed the manner of English and he tried to point out the very precise, vivid feeling using the Japanese language very clearly. It is such a different way of explaining and using Japanese, within the context of a poem or short essay. His attitude, I really appreciate it. It's very sharp, opening it up and presenting it. It's very modern, very dry, in a way several meanings and layers in one word, one poem which is quite..., very emotional, but not too emotional. What he presented was very astute and straight and contemporary — harsh. I know he wanted to be an industrial designer. The way of thinking is like a designer's way of thinking, fitting into a designer's way.

Tomoko: That's maybe why we feel sympathy.

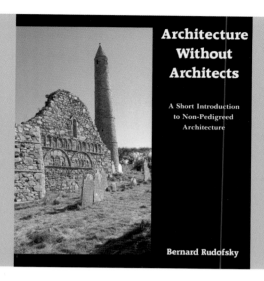

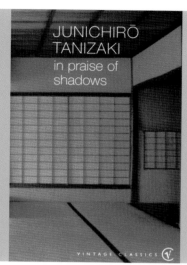

Bernard Rudofsky,
Architecture Without Architects,
book jacket, 1964

Junichiro Tanizaki,
In Praise of Shadows,
book jacket, 1933

cars

Shin: I don't have any attachment to cars honestly.

Tomoko: I have no attachment. It's the Tube that brings me quicker than I can walk. I have no feeling for cars.

Shin: I don't care at all.

Lem Bar Stool, 2000
HM 30 Sofa, 2001.

Donkey 3, 2003

Shin: Actually, I was making films until the age of 20. I wanted to be an animation director. My hero at that time was Norman McLaren. He's another Canadian. At that time, the Canadian National Film Board was subsidising quite a lot of animators, a lot of interesting people like Norman McLaren and the Indian animator, Ishu Patel. McLaren's interests were simple — the synchronisation of picture and sound. He played with lots of different methods. When I saw his film there was a balance between the entertaining aspect and the experimental aspect. That was absolutely well balanced. His films are very experimental and never boring, because with the sound and movement they are so amusing.

Tomoko: It is something very delicate and funny. You are always smiling when you watch his films.

Shin: He is a master of a mix of disciplines — choreography, directing, writing scratching on to the film, creating and synchronising the sound. The scratch is visual, and sometimes he scratches onto the soundtrack as well. He creates funny sounds with his scratch, and also creates an orchestral sound and scratch sound combination. It is very interesting. My favourite film from him is *Canon*. He created these three different sequences based on the Canon music, overlapping the melody again and again and again. For example, in one, there is a part of the sequence from *Canon*. And these individual characters are following the exact same kind of route but while following this kind of movement they are overlapping together, but it never touches, never crashes, continuing, so well composed, very interesting. When we developed, for example, our table=chest furniture piece or the armchair=table, we always had the visual image of *Canon*. That comes back to me because the armchair=table is really structured in a way that it is almost touching, rotating, floating, but never touches never crashes, and then opens so the movement of an armchair becomes a table for us. This has really close links to the Norman McLaren films. I don't know how directly people see the connection, but we are always thinking about the movement and direction which is happening in animation and film. Also the balance between the experimental and entertainment that he presents is so real. We always try to create a balance between the entertaining aspect of design and the experimental aspects of design.

Tomoko: For me it is a bit different. My favourite film is *Delicatessen*. I'm amazed by how the director made space that you can feel within this film. It is like *Star Wars*, you see a huge space on the screen, but it is not human scale at all. In *Delicatessen*, the story is within one building. Somebody lives in the basement, the vegetarians are on the ground floor, then the butchers, and then the lodgers. It is connected really organically and the story is always concerned with the people within the building and how they think about

Shin and Tomoko Azumi

someone who is living below them. The way the space is connected by pipes and walls and sounds and waters makes it very interesting for me. And in a similar sense, Kurosawa's *Yojimbo* is another film which I like. It's a story within a small village, and *Yojimbo* is a god who is employed by two power groups.

Shin: That film is almost like a western movie.

Tomoko: The two parties in the small village are always fighting against each other. God is always taking his place on the top of a tower and watching what the two parties are doing. So, it's a very small space but very three-dimensional. Only that suggestion gives you the perspective of human beings, small things. There are activities that are shown through a birds-eye view, which is an interesting way of looking — so, in a similar sense, I like that.

Jean-Pierre Jeunet, Delicatessen, promotional postcard, 1990

Tomoko: I like James Turrell's work. His way of using light is amazing. It's always an illusion and abstract and always talking about space, which I like. I like Mario Merz, as well.

Shin: So difficult, so many names.

Tomoko: I like Mona Hatoum, too.

Shin: I like quite a lot of artists, but I wouldn't focus on one. Norman McLaren, he's an artist and he's one of my favourite artists, but if I narrow it down to fine artists, who do I like? Maybe Anish Kapoor, I like him, but not that deep. Oscar Schlemmer, one of the Bauhaus teachers, who created a series of mechanical ballets that are very abstract is one of my favourites. He could be described as an artist or a director or a sculptor. I'm more interested in kinetic artists like Jean Tinguely. He's my favourite artist. Susumu Shingu is another of my favourite artists. He's a sculptor, he creates a window pane sculpture that moves with air. I really like kinetic things. I'm not so much interested in static things. What I like is the spirit of kinetic. I think he also took part in Expo 70.

Tomoko: That's a big thing for us. We were five years old!

Shin: Very smoothly. The movement of these sculptures is very unexpected and unpredictable. From my childhood I have been watching this sculpture moving in the wind. I couldn't believe this was moving with just the wind because it looks so heavy and chunky, but it moves just with wind.

Tomoko: You can see Susumu Shingu kinetic sculptures, just below the ceiling, at the Japanese National Airport.

Shin: He had a great exhibition when I was about 19 years old. The title was *Breathing Sculpture*. All his works were not chunky but made out of paper and canvas, very thin sculpture all installed within this gallery. They were very delicate and caught the subtle movement of air within a room, whether because of air conditioning or because of open windows. It shows the kind of movement — air with the sculpture. I've always liked something with movement, which makes me happy and warm.

Shin and Tomoko Azumi

Comb Chair, 2004

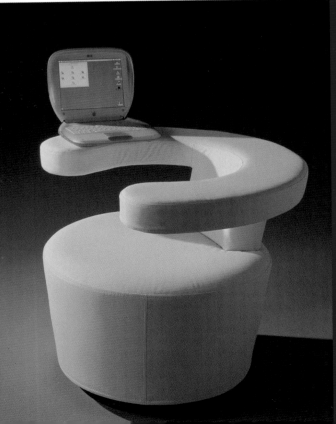

ShipShape, 2003

Big Arm, 2000

Orbital workstation, 2003

Z A Angle, 2004

Shin and Tomoko Azumi

press

Tomoko: We use press for every project. We do as much as we can widely, so we subscribe to *Blueprint* and *Elle Décor* because we want to cover commercial to academic.

Shin: We always want to check if someone has done a similar idea before us.

Tomoko: We have to stop if we find something like that.

Shin: Or go over it.

Tomoko: For us magazines are for checking the market in the world.

people

Tomoko: Coco Chanel, she has been revolutionary.

Shin: Thomas Edison.

Tomoko and Shin: Issey Miyake, we met him on the street last week in Tokyo and we shook hands.

Shin: Jamie Oliver.

Shin and Tomoko Azumi 47

Ronan and Erwan Bouroullec

Ronan and Erwan Bouroullec were born in Quimper, France, in 1971 and 1976, respectively. Upon graduating from the Ecole Nationale des Arts Décoratifs in Paris, Ronan began working alone, progressively assisted by Erwan, still a student at the Ecole des Beaux-Arts at Cergy Pontoise. The two brothers have been working together since 1999. Their collaboration is a constant dialogue, nourished by their personal identities striving towards a common goal.

Ronan and Erwan Bouroullec work with numerous manufacturers, such as Vitra, Cappellini, Issey Miyake, Magis, Ligne Roset and Habitat. At the same time, they have undertaken other projects, like the Floating House, an artists studio commissioned by Le centre d'Art de Chatou, and conceived in collaboration with architects Denis Daversin and Jean-Marie Finot.

Awarded Creators of the Year at the Salon du Meuble in Paris, 2002, they have won multiple awards such as the New Designer Award at the International Furniture Fair of New York, le Grand Prix du Design de la Ville de Paris, and the First Prize at the Saint-Etienne Biennale. In 2003, they were elected Designer of

Lit Clos Bed, 2000

Ronan: For me, if we go back some years, I think we were very impressed by Italian designers in general, particularly those of the 1960s and 70s. We admired designers like Ettore Sottsass and other Italian designers, but for different reasons. First, maybe it was because of Sottsass' success, maybe for his ability to play in different ways at the same time, and also at the way he could balance industrial projects for, say, Olivetti, but at the same time spend ten weeks in India working on precise craft objects. In terms of designers today, we are very close to Andrea Branzi. We loved his book *Domestic Animals*. In terms of sensational design, we like Achille Castiglioni and...

Erwan: ... people like Bruno Munari.

Ronan: Yes, Bruno Munari. In terms of our influences, they are not related solely to form as a direct influence, but it is in terms of the spirit of the designers and the way in which they consider things, and the angle they take in approaching a project. I think there are some interesting developments in design at the moment. The first thing, maybe, is that for industrial design, particularly for big companies that have their own in-house design studio, I think they understand that there is an interest to try to work with different entities of design — namely smaller design groups. So, for our design studio here, we sometimes work for really big companies and sometimes for small craftsmen. It is important that we understand that it is possible and important to work in different ways. At the end of the day we can learn that a craftsman's approach can be very interesting to integrate into industrial processes, and we can say the same thing for the big industry. What we learn in an industrial context can be very interesting to the craft approach.

Erwan: We are in a time in which products and things in general can be more and more precise, whereas the things produced in the 60s and 70s attempted to fit nearly anyone, anywhere. Because of globalisation, large organisations, in general, give the impression that they have imposed economically efficient ways of thinking about things. Finally, this has generated a lot of different groups of people, who are interested in many different things. So we can make more and more precise products for precise people. That is why design is more and more visible nowadays, because the objects are more and more precise and defined, and this is why they impress the eyes a little bit more than in the 60s or 70s.

Ronan: I think, generally, we try to take pleasure in our work. I think I am more or less a hedonist at the end of the day, so I try to play a lot.

Erwan: We never try to get away from the real simplicity of an object. We like to add little things together and at the end we have this complex landscape on which you can discover small things.

What is interesting about design is that you always have to have a dialogue when you make something. You draw it and then you have to find someone to make it, someone to pack it and someone to sell it. And every time, people ask us this same question: "Isn't it too difficult to make something?" But for us it is not a problem of difficulty. The thing that is interesting is that we are not the only people involved in the project.

That is why design is more and more visible nowadays, because the objects are more and more precise and defined, and this is why they impress the eyes a little bit more than in the 60s or 70s.

Achille and Pier Giacomo Castiglioni, Mezzadro Stool, 1957

Enzo Mari, Box Chair, 1975-1976

Ronan and Erwan Bouroullec

BETC, 2002

Ronan and Erwan Bouroullec

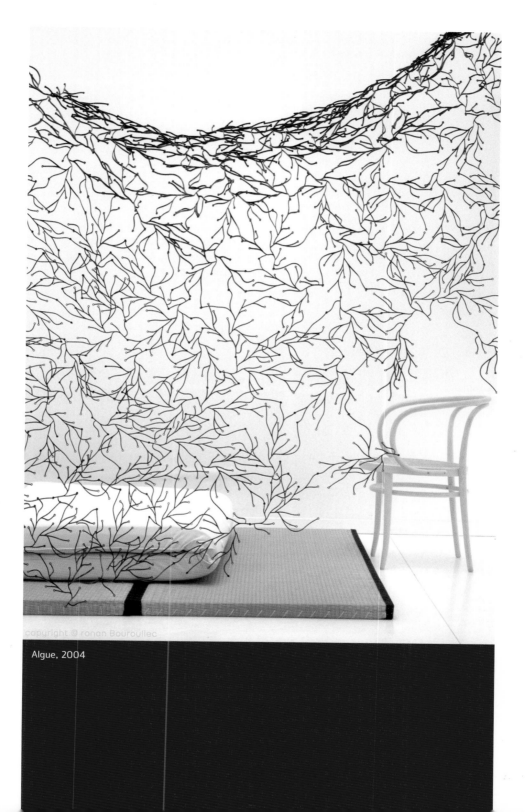

Algue, 2004

Assemblage, 2004

Algue, 2004

Algue, 2004

Ronan and Erwan Bouroullec

Erwan: I am always fed up with big architecture and big things. I am only interested in a programme that could be called "the urban landscape". When you simply walk into, and are confronted by, different things in an urban landscape, like Tokyo, it is really beautiful because everything is different. You can have two hours that stick together that have no routes. Sometimes there is this kind of jungle because they have, I think, big problems with electric wires and telephones and at the same time everywhere there is vegetation, plants growing. I love to walk in the city. Of course, there are some places that we would go more than others but they should be discovered through walking, it is not some kind of defined place. Sometimes a place can be really beautiful because you get out of the tube and there is just a tree there, and if you get out at the other exit of the tube, you just go directly onto a road. So the place is not as beautiful as the experience.

Ronan: There are two cities for me that are really interesting in this accidental way. The first is Rome and the second Lisbon. For very simple reasons, I think more and more if we look at the centre of all the big cities in Europe, they have nearly all become really similar — same shops, same signage. In Rome and Lisbon, however, you can always find a little shop in which you can buy some very utilitarian things.

Erwan: And then you find just next to this shop a shop which sells some decorative things, but after that there is a shop selling some taps.

Ronan: The landscapes of the shops are very different, because their interior layout does not come from a marketing manual. At the moment I am a little bit terrified with these new commercial centres.

Erwan: We also have another strong story of 'sea landscapes', as we come from Brittany and we used to surf. There is something funny when you surf. You have to get the right waves, you always have to follow the time of the sea, and you have to marry it as it moves during the day. Sometimes you go surfing at seven in the morning because it is right for waves. And if you stay in the same place for two weeks, the time will have changed and the best time for surfing will be around ten in the evening, just because it moves every day. Here around the city, it is not the sea, but it's more, just to get some waves, which means that sometimes you can get some waves in some quite strange places and there is always this kind of eroded architecture because of the wind or sand, like pill boxes. At the start of World War Two they were at the top of the beach, but the sea always eats the beach, so now all the pill boxes are inside the sea. They are a quite strange kind of building.

Ronan: In Rome and Lisbon there is really a culture, a way of life, and not a culture of a marketing way of life. When you are in Lisbon or Rome, and when you decide to eat something you can always find a little place with quality, but not with marketing quality. So, there is this kind of nostalgia, this culture of doing something, this culture of taking coffee. Low cost, because last September in Lisbon coffee was the equivalent of 25 cents — 25 cents, it's nothing. It is the same price if you are inside or outside the cafe. It is not only a commercial question. It's more a culture of doing something. Doing something in a good way, in terms of life and not in terms of making money.

Erwan: It is not only a question of making money, because in Paris there are a lot of great places. However, when there is a bar in Paris it has to be a special bar. I have the impression that in Lisbon it is much less, it is not so important. Also here, in St Denis, is quite an interesting place. Perhaps St Denis is not a pleasant place, and probably I would prefer to live in Paris. What is here, though, is that there are so many people coming from everywhere. They are not very rich people. There are also some quite 'upper class' people in St Denis, but there are many quite poor people. All this mix of things means that the place is totally uncontrolled, and sometimes it can get really dirty and sometimes it can get really clean. And sometimes you can find one or two good shops and, perhaps, after one year they will have changed to selling cheap things, and then it will continue to change.

Ronan: It is not a corporate place.

Erwan: You know, here there are many Moroccan shops selling beers and things, they serve big plates of cous cous, and they sell strange decorations which come from their country and are very inexpensive. That is really interesting, and that is what makes this place a big city.

Tokyo Streetscape, 2002

Ronan and Erwan Bouroullec

Erwan: There is a product, a lamp from Castiglioni, which I especially like because a lot of his projects look as if they are ready-made. In many of his products he linked existing things and made some small changes and brought just enough poetry out of them. I have got a lamp, it is really well known, which is a small lamp and under it is a round plate. He made a part of it sand-blasted, and the light bulb is transparent which makes the light softer. The round plate underneath is an old cinema tape holder, and for me it reaches quite a high level of poetry. It is linguistic really, a lot of cleverness about industry and producing something. Perhaps this is a good reference for me.

There is always this problem in design. Sometimes design can mean progress, but design can become an object just like a Gucci thing. We are totally fighting against this kind of thing. We are really interested in landscapes, mixed landscapes, and quite often some products are just beautiful because they remind you of an already existing product, or because they are some kind of mirror of an object, or because they are just inserted into a range of objects. And for us to say one product or another is a little difficult because we like diversity and mix, everything makes sense together and not alone.

Ronan: I don't read a lot. Sometimes when I decide to read I go in a lot of different directions. I like, particularly, to read the newspaper, especially the politics section. My favourite writer, however, is Emile Zola.

Erwan: I read quite a lot of science fiction. Philip K Dick is quite interesting. In general I have always been a science fiction fan. There is another part of science fiction that I follow, which is the science fiction book in which someone is imagining a world order. And so, the author will try to describe everything, and sometimes it is quite interesting because it touches on all the writings of the seventeenth and eighteenth centuries.

Ronan: Especially Jules Verne.

Philip K Dick,
Do Androids Dream of Electric Sheep?,
book jacket, 1968

Jules Verne,
Twenty Thousand Leagues Under the Sea,
book jacket, 1869

BETC, 2002

BETC, 2002

60 Ronan and Erwan Bouroullec

Cabane, 2001

TV Vase, 2001

Ronan and Erwan Bouroullec

Ronan: For us there is not a big project or a small project. If we work on an ashtray or on a car it is the same question.

Erwan: You know we both have a Porsche. Sometimes it's the woman that gets into the car that makes you love the car. It can be a problem.

Ronan: For me, maybe the Fiat, the little Fiat Cinquecento. The old one.

Erwan: For me it is the famous car, which was called the Mehari. It is a French car manufactured by Citroën. I think the Citroën Mehari was more or less the same idea as the 2CV in that you could open everything. It was a cross between a 2CV and a Jeep, and it is really cheap on energy and cheap on metal.

You know we both have a Porsche. Sometimes it's the woman that gets into the car that makes you love the car. It can be a problem.

Citroën Mehari, c. 1970

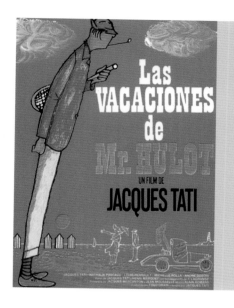

Jacques Tati,
Las Vacaciones de Mr Hulot,
promotional postcard, 1954

Federico Fellini, 8 1/2,
promotional postcard, 1963

Ronan: I really like the old westerns of John Ford, although not all of them. I really like the way he did landscapes and the ability he had to translate the landscape. After that I would say Jim Jarmusch's movie *Strangers in Paradise,* or a film like that. Also Jaques Tati, Akira Kurosawa and Takeshi Kitano.

Erwan: For me, it's a big problem because I never remember the name of an actor or a movie. I remember, more, quite a lot of documentary films. I saw a documentary recently, which featured the Chicago suburbs and some poor black servants. It is a three hour documentary without any commentary, just filming people, and yes, it was interesting and strong.

Ronan: I like film, especially for the sound.

Erwan: Ah, yes, there is something I like probably more for the music at the end and it is *Paris, Texas*. You know he looks for this woman during the entire movie, and you get into this kind of sexy thing in which she is in front of the mirror and he is on the other side of the mirror.

artists

Erwan: We've always felt very free with art. Free to look, free to like, free to dislike, free to make. And me especially, I never learnt any design when I was in school. I was in art school, at which I made paintings and other things, many things. And for me art has probably influenced me more, as totally different from what I could do and what I could like — it has always opened the field, and opened the past. And, so, my influence list is quite large. It goes from artists like Malcolm Morley in the USA, and this strong story of American paintings,... and also Frank Stella.

Ronan: For me, maybe if I have to say this one and this one, I would list Donald Judd and, in the same way, I would also say the landscapes of Gerhard Richter.

Malcolm Morley, Blue Burka, 2002

Ronan and Erwan Bouroullec

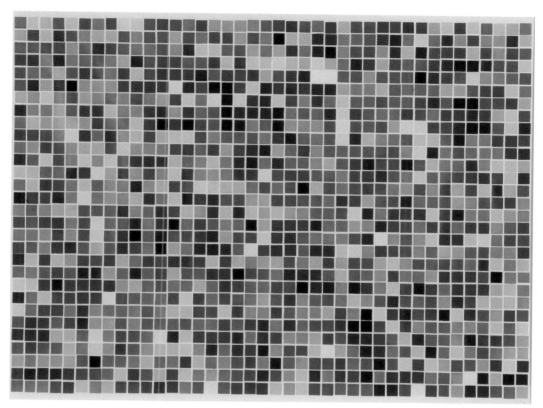

Gerhard Richter, Colour Fields, 1973

Ronan: For me, I am not influenced by music at all.

Erwan: For me, when I was younger, I followed the English group called The Wedding Present. I also used to really like the band called My Bloody Valentine.

Ronan: I think we were all interested in the story of The Stone Roses, perhaps because of the link with the British scene.

Erwan: But now with music, I don't understand why there is always this idea of the music and, I think, some kind of bad rules, saying the only way to make music is if you can make it with a real guitar and that if you cannot play the music in a gig, then it is not real music. That is really a small point of view on music. And, so, I just passed along without ever really listening to music, some reggae, some jazz, some electronic music. I just did not understand that my interest was really growing at this stage and I wanted to know more and more. I have tried to find a lot of different music genres. Now I listen to, it is not salsa *per se*, but a 'low' music with girls singing from South America. It has a good rhythm.

The Stone Roses, Second Coming,
CD cover, 1994

Ronan: For newspapers, I prefer the French newspaper *Le Monde*.

Erwan: I think it is a good newspaper. *Le Monde* is a serious newspaper.

Ronan: It is more to the left, in terms of politics, but it is progressive, so it is not too excessive. We read a lot of magazines, we look at some pictures in magazines, and sometimes we read them when we can. *Domus* for example.

Erwan: Me, I don't especially read magazines, not too much. Newspapers, not so much, but I used to read something that became a monthly thing about music, which was called *Les Inrockuptibles*. In this magazine you would find all these long interviews of a lot of young people making music, and also people coming from the cinema. And, so, it was really something like my bible. Finally, we got an article in it two weeks ago, but in the design part.

Erwan: Napoleon or Stalin, perhaps.

Ronan: Yesterday, I was at a dinner party, so that is why I am a little bit tired. I was with Mark Newson and Jasper Morrison.

Erwan: For me, I would quite like to meet with an astrophysicist. You know the kind of people who know everything about the universe. They know really precise details about every physical thing. Some quantum physicist, but not Einstein. Perhaps, as there is all this chaos theory, you know during the 1950s and 60s, I would like to meet with an astrophysicist.

Matali Crasset

Matali Crasset was born in 1965 in Châlons-en-Champagne. After graduating at the Ateliers Ecole Nationale Supérieure de Création Industrielle (ENSCI), she worked with Denis Santachiara in Milan, on architecture, design and exhibition projects. On her return to Paris, she worked with Philippe Starck at Thomson Multimedia, where she became responsible for Tim Thom, Thomson's design centre.

Having continued to develop her own projects alongside her work for Starck, Crasset opened her own studio in Paris in 1998. She now works across a wide range of disciplines on mass-manufactured furniture and electronic products, as well as more experimental projects.

She has created products and furniture for a number of manufacturers, including Authentics, Domodinamica, Lexon, Orangina, Seb and s.m.a.k., and has been awarded the Grand Prix du Design of the City of Paris, and the Sue Ryder Foundation commissioned her to create the church furniture for the Maison de Marie chapel, Lourdes.

Matali Crasset is regularly invited as a Visiting Lecturer at design schools throughout France and abroad, including Les Ateliers in Paris, and the Domus Academy, Milan.

Oritapi Carpet Game, 1999

If I were talking about the past I would say Joe Colombo. I like how he worked with various typologies of furniture, and also space, and he is so very, very free and going on different fields all the time. So, I think he is quite open-minded, and for me it's the same for Verner Panton. As for the designers of today, I mean it's more complex because I am more interested by the way designers think than the results, and I am afraid that I would say that my references are more diverse than solely the field of design. It is also art and music, it is references that are much more widespread than the field of design.

Travel, for example, is a way to take a little bit and be away from your thinking and to have the ability to think more about your personal day to day life. And I think it's very important for that. It's very interesting because each time you find a way to think that differently you get different ideas. But the pity right now, when you go to the big cities, like Moscow, is that there is not so much difference. All the cities are a little bit similar. All the shops you can find in one or another place, or you have to look very closely in that place to find the differences in the culture. It means you need more time, and if you study for only one week, you could remain at the superficial level of that city and never understand the culture of the place. So, what I like is to stay in a city and to understand it from the inside, and be in contact with the people living in the city. To have a shortcut, so you can understand more about the culture. It can help us to see how people live in different ways and in the best space. In a way, it is like a mirror and you find a way to think about your work and how you can make your work evolve.

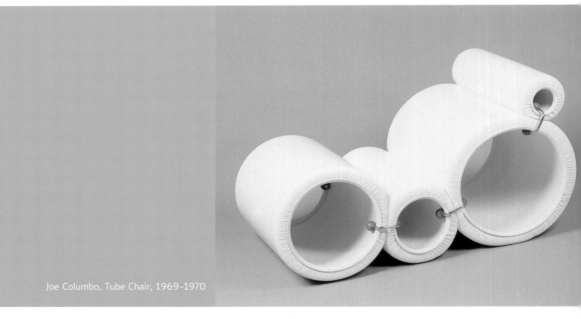

Joe Columbo, Tube Chair, 1969-1970

Matali Crasset

... the pity right now, when you go to the big cities, like Moscow, is that there is not so much difference. All the cities are a little bit similar. All the shops you can find in one or another place, or you have to look very closely in that place to find the differences in the culture.

buildings

We had an exhibition of Oscar Niemeyer in Paris recently, which I went to. I was very impressed by not only how Niemeyer did the space, but more by how you felt in it. The main idea when inside was to feel outside. He made an irregular floor, and when you went into this building you felt like it was outside. It's a very simple idea, but it worked really well. So I was very interested by this simple idea, which brought something very comfortable. A way to feel the space in a comfortable way. I have seen similar projects in Sao Pāulo created by Niemeyer, and, in any case, I am not impressed by the façade, but how you feel inside and the simple ideas that can make you feel like you are in a different place. I think Niemeyer adopts more of a human approach than a purely aesthetic approach in his work, which I admire.

Mobiwork Workspace, 2001

Bath, HI Hotel, Nice, 2003

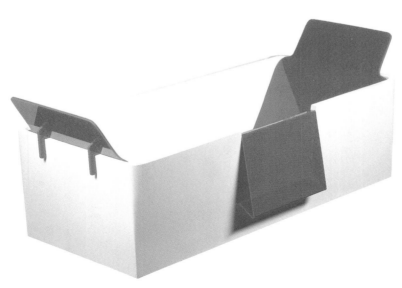

Matali Crasset

Happy Bar, HI Hotel, Nice, 2003

It's more about the objects I have collected when I was working with Phillipe Starck. I am not so interested in buying objects. I am less and less interested in collecting products now than I was in the past. I am more interested in, like, making a teapot of things, very different things. Some of the objects I have been working on here are prototypes, and others are more like children's toys. I don't care about having a sophisticated place, with the exact product to use. More and more, I try to be less influenced by things around me. But the objects I have collected little by little, they belong to my story in a way.

I am more interested by the way designers think nowadays. As designers, we have the productivity to create objects, not only focusing on the response to the aesthetic, but the construction, how things work and the typology of things. I think the objects I like more work on those kinds of levels. During the 60s, for example, the work of the group Archigram showed that there was much greater freedom to express all kinds of connections between different things at home, or the idea of living on the pavement, all kinds of ideas like that. I am much more interested in this kind of object, because this type of process and thinking is much more related to my own process of thinking. But right now you have many more possibilities. We have all kinds of new materials today, so in a way I feel more connected to these people in the 60s than I do today, because of their way of thinking. It's hard to explain, but I think it's a bit like that.

I am currently doing a lot of exhibition design and using a lot of inflatable objects. So I try to, little by little, find different ways of making structures. It's a process of using references. Today's projects are more concerned with aesthetic issues. When I went to the last Milan show, I was a little disappointed because all the ideas were about 'pop'. Popular, but in the way of colours, but not in the way of how to connect things, how to make the design a different kind of proposal. I was a little bit disappointed, even, by the big companies that are, in a way, advanced and working on this type of connection, but were concentrating on the aesthetic. In France we always have the problem that decoration is very strong, and if you want the design to be much more, you have to break, to say, "Stop!" And say, "we have to concentrate on a different way to see it, to live". When you look at people, how the clothes on people are very different from ten years ago, and when you look at how the people live it's the same structure. In each house we have the sofa, and in front of the sofa is the TV, and it's generally like that. I think strongly that, as a designer, we have to propose and make the way we live evolve, and not just around shapes and beautiful objects. But it's very complicated, because people rate an object first through shape and aesthetic traits. They have always done that. It's a type of process, and it will take some time to be accepted. So, I'm always looking at different fields, how artists can give sensation and feelings to their pieces, and also how sociologists are explaining the mentality — the way we think.

Matali Crasset

One thing that strikes me is the Office-Bed for the Workspheres exhibition by Hella Jongerius, which shows a very different way of working. I am also interested in how we integrate technology and how we can domesticate technology. Because right now it's like we take a new technology that's not finished, but it is given to the consumer, the user. So I think we have a big role to play in domesticating technology and making it seem more comfortable and more human in a way. That's why I enjoyed working with Philippe Starck a lot on the Thomson projects, because it was the beginning of this kind of area of concern. And now industry is quite afraid. People want something different, people do not simply accept feelings like that now. The consumer is becoming more mature, and the industry, as a consequence, has to take care and be much more responsive. So, I think it will become more interesting pretty soon, because consumers and manufacturers will have war, perhaps with the designer, and we will design not only aesthetic objects.

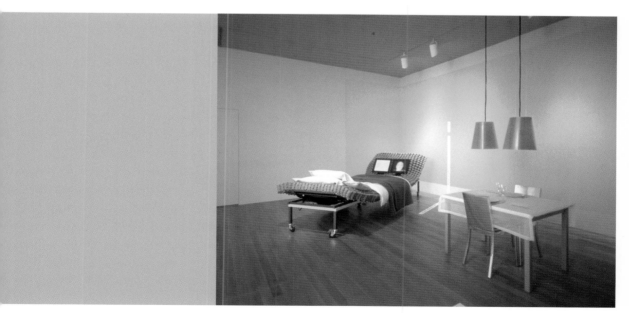

Hella Jongerius, My Soft Office-Bed in Business for MOMA Workspheres Exhibition, 2000

Matali Crasset 75

I am always interested in the idea of taking materials, of having something to think about, and making my work evolve in a way I didn't know. Sometimes it is very indirect. It is not direct. We, in France, have really good theorists right now. They are in-between philosophers and anthropologists, and so, are very interesting. In the past, I read a lot also. The author I was looking for is Georges Perec. He is also French. Perec was a guy who described a very simple way of living everyday life. For example, he made a book on describing a person sleeping. He made all kinds of things like that, or he wrote a book around the life of a house with different connections between people. I am much more interested in work like this. Then you have Baudrillard, and all the French theoreticians. But Perec is more about literature, and more about day to day life. I don't know how you can describe his work adequately....

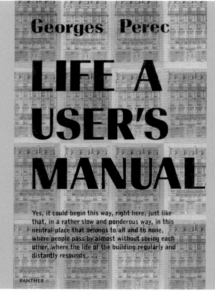

Jean Baudrillard,
The Spirit of Terrorism,
book jacket, 2002

Georges Perec,
Life A User's Manual,
book jacket, 1978

I am not so interested in cars, because they are much more a support for power than a means of transportation right now. When they truly becomes a means of transport I will be much more interested in these objects. No, I look at cars, but I don't feel attracted to them. Sometimes there is a concept that could be interesting, but usually the energy dissipates because the car industry is not ready to lose this idea of status, or power. They are not ready for this concept, so the industry is trying, in a way, to show things differently. It is always grim. I hope, that pretty soon, we can become intelligent enough to have cars that are 'responsible'.

Like everybody, I was very surprised by the number of people who rollerblade in the city. When you see a group of people all wearing rollerblades going through the streets of Paris, this is something that was impossible a few years ago. So, I am much more interested by this kind of evolution than I am in car design.

And it's not a fashion. I think when you try it, it's a bit like the bicycle. It lets you go, and you feel free in the city. You feel the city in a very different way. The city suddenly becomes yours. I think this is more interesting for individuals, and a very simple way to move around the city. It is like an extension of the body that gives you power. We had to gain it back. I think we've gone too far in the other way.

> I am not so interested in cars, because they are much more a support for power than a means of transportation right now.

I like the work of Jacques Demy, a French director. He made comedies, French comedies, which is quite unusual. He made a famous film — certainly in France — called *Les Demoiselles de Rochefort*. I like this movie because it gives you a lot of optimism, and this film was meant to be courageous. Also, he is a very clever guy because he had an idea that changing the day to day lives of people makes people active. It was the first film that really encouraged women to be active, and so Demy gave them clothes that were more in the spirit of sportswear than everyday streetwear. And people like colour, and when they see colour they become optimistic. It is fresh, and it's a way of showing the side to life. The film was made around 1960, or between 1950 and 1960. In a way it's very French but it is, how could I explain this, something of a French cartoon, it's very difficult to explain. Jacques Demy was very influenced by American comedies, but he succeeded in making comedies with a French style to them. And perhaps this idea of optimism, when you look at this film, makes you stronger and encourages you to be good in life. And I think this is very important.

I would like, in a way, with my design work, to do the same. You know, to give people optimism and to show them that life is worth living. I think we really exist right now in a period where there are a lot of events taking place and you miss their references. I think it's very important to feel comfortable in your surroundings. I try, with my furniture, or with the spaces I am making, to provide an opportunity to make a 'structure' so as to have separate relationships with others. I am working right now on a new concept for a hotel in Nice on the Côte d'Azur. The concept is based on an idea of experimenting with space, within the normal boundaries of a hotel. So, we have eight different bedroom concepts, and we consider the space to be like a network, and we have connections with people making music, and people making images. So, it's like, people come there to be very active, and to be curious and, yeah, I would like the people to become more curious about how they live.

artists

I like video art. I am very interested in the work of Bill Viola, for example. Who else would I say? Ernesto Neto. He created a very good exhibition in a gallery in Paris. He created a space, and he used foam, big pieces of foam. And he did, like, a gallery inside the gallery by putting in tunnels, you know, just to experiment with, like when you were a child. The use of this material is quite nice, because the light passes through it. It's very intelligent. Neto works with one material at a time like that. It could be cardboard, it could be foam, but each time it is very sensitive and very efficient. And I like artists who make good connections between their art and people, and who see their work as a functional thing that does something when you use it. Neto made this exhibition using great colours, and shapes. He placed spices inside a structure for the *Venice Biennale* recently. So, when you enter the space something very strange happens, and you feel, with the spices, you feel the space. I like the idea of all this stimuli — not only visual, but global stimuli that transports you more than a merely visual thing.

press

Depending upon how much time I have, as I can be very busy, I usually go through papers very quickly. I receive daily newspapers like *Le Liberation*, so we look a little bit at the global news. I look at art magazines more, because I like to look at what's going on in the art world.

Right now there are a lot of new magazines that are not saying much, you know, very experimental ones. They are like fanzines. I like these kinds of magazines, because I think there is really a kind of freedom to them, you know. There is no advertising, and so you can be sure the content is more free, in a way. And you also find more experimental things in this type of publication. In a way, when you look at magazines right now it is like there is one way to make pictures. There are fashion-type photographers and photographs. And creativity is lost, in a way. So you have to find your own way with small magazines, to find out what is going on in the mainstream. I think the innovation is really coming from the very small magazines, and little by little big enterprises are taking them over and making them commercial objects.

"Permis de construire", 2000

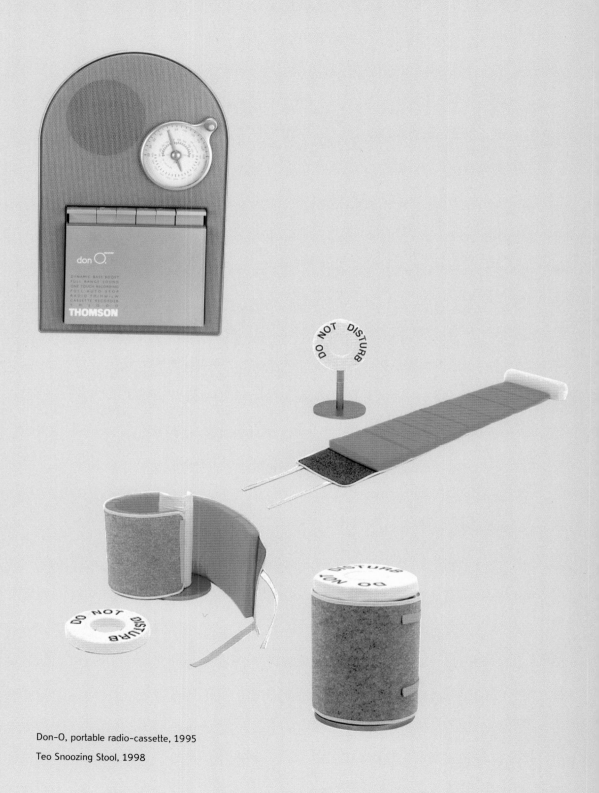

Don-O, portable radio-cassette, 1995

Teo Snoozing Stool, 1998

I am very interested in how music democratises people through using the tools of the computer and the web. Look at how musicians are working. They take a piece of classical music, they take a piece of noise, and they use all of the material they can find around them. And when you make a comparison with how we work as designers, we can't work like this. It's kind of forbidden. It's like breaking all the rules and providing to everybody with possibilities. That is why I am talking about democratisation. And I think it's very interesting, what's going on in music right now. It's related to patience. Everybody has the opportunity to approach music. Before, you needed to take lessons, to work hard and learn music for say two to three years, so people were excluded from music. Let's take an example. Even if you don't like classical music, I am sure you can find somebody who works with classical music who mixes it with, I don't know, African music. And, in a way, you enter into the classical way, and I think this allows you to be in contact with many different things than previously. Like being more interested in jazz than classical, which was, sort of, forbidden. It was like the imposition of what kind of music you could listen to. It's difficult to understand.

In the past I listened to a lot of industrial music. So, I was much more concerned with the Berlin scene, and the German scene in general. I liked the music of Kraftwerk. They sometimes make music that is quite hard, cold and repetitive. And, in a way, I was prepared for what is going on now with techno, because for ten years I was already listening to similar sounds in Berlin. I feel comfortable with that kind of music.

I am very interested in how music democratises people through using the tools of the computer and the web.

Matali Crasset

people

It's very complicated to admire a person for their work. You know what I mean? I have tried to find one and I am not quite sure I have succeeded in this.

I think if I could find a guy like Jacques Demy — he is dead now, but I would be interested in asking him things about his films so as to understand their structure, to understand more about his idea of making people happy. But you know, I would be much more interested in having a dinner with the people who have helped me to evolve in my life, and that would include Phillipe Starck. Because I have never really had the opportunity to discuss things with him on a one to one basis I would like to have dinner with him one day to thank him for what he gave to me. Yeah, I have been thinking of this. And I'd also like to invite the people who have given me something simple that that changed my life. You know, I haven't always been working within design culture. I came from a small village where there was no art association or theatre. Little by little I was trying to find 'culture' and along this road I have had the opportunity of meeting people who showed me that it was possible to become a designer. So, sometimes these people were not artists at all but people who have allowed me to have this luxury, because I think it is a luxury to do this job and become a creative person.

Nick Crosbie

Nick Crosbie established Inflate in 1995 and is now the company's Creative Director. Inflate started life with a small range of inflatable household products and has now evolved into one of the UK's most recognised design studios. With the own brand product range still at the heart of the studio's focus, Crosbie and his creative team now work on a plethora of client projects, ranging from products and packaging through to architecture.

The studio's consultancy work lists clients such as Boots, Habitat, Selfridges, O2, and Virgin Atlantic. Over the years the studio has collaborated with other leading designers, including Michael Marriott, Michael Young, and Ron Arad. The company has been the recipient of several design awards including the 100% Design/Blueprint Award for their inflatable Table light and the Peugeot Design Award for their Snoozy bed.

The Inflate product collection has worldwide distribution and the studio have been invited to hold numerous international exhibitions and events to promote their work, including a solo show at the Victoria and Albert Museum in London.

The studio now have an 'own brand' store in London and a book entitled *I'll Keep Thinking*, by Black Dog Publishing, was recently published, detailing more of Crosbie and his studio's work.

birdhouse

Birdhouse, 2002

I only really started designing in 1989, and the first designs I ever saw was the work of Mark Newson during a trip to Spain. I bought a magazine and his work was in it. It was one of the first pieces of 'design' I remember. More recently, and since I started Inflate, I have learnt a lot more about designers — you start to understand more about objects. When I see an object now I read more into it, I understand more about the designers — you realise that it's not just about how things look, it's about the ideas behind them. That's what I look for now.

The designers I find really interesting — and they are very influential to me now — are Charles and Ray Eames. I admire the way that they embraced new technology and how they developed ideas from that, and learnt how things were made and tried to push the boundaries of what could be done. In early plywood furniture, you couldn't make compound curves, but they worked out ways to do it. They themselves experimented, this wasn't done by the factory. The Eames' made all their furniture jigs in their workshop, and this is what we try to do with whatever plastic process we're working with here at Inflate. We try to learn about materials and process, and we try to push this. We can see what is going on and we try to push it, to see if we can open up more potential, just as the Eames' would have done. I admire Ray Eames's spirit, her creativity. She was very interested in the emotional side of things. Whereas Charles Eames was much more interested in the process, pushing it and making it work. Ray was much more interested in the emotional side of design, which is hard to harness with machinery.

And if you look at people who are working now, such as Ingo Maurer; he is an interesting designer in that he has managed to stick with his own ideas through all sorts of different fashions. Since the 1960s, as fashion has gone up and down, he has stuck with his vision. And I would like that for ourselves here at Inflate. When we first started, in 1995, we were very fashionable because we were working with plastics. Plastic was very trendy back then and we were caught up in this, which was a nightmare, because if you are taken up by 'fashion', then once fashion disappears, you come crashing down. We spent a couple of years coming back down and just surviving and doing new stuff. Now I feel I don't want fashion. I want a solid core idea that runs irrespective of what's going on outside, is always in demand and is running in its own way. But a lot of designers are very fashionable and work with fashion. Fashion is a very temperamental part of the industry to work with — I've seen this first-hand.

Philippe Stark became very famous as a result of the French government sponsoring contemporary design within French culture. Newson has modelled himself much closer to a pop star and became a brand in his own right. Newson is a brand. It's like sticking Nike on something. I don't know how it is going to pan out for him. It really depends where he moves next. For Starck, it was hard because during the late 1980s and early 90s, with all the work he was doing for Alessi and Flos, he became massive, and there comes a point when you struggle to reinvent yourself. He's done some weird things, and that's what happens when you have to push yourself. You almost want to fail, so you can learn something. He knows full well he can design a coffee maker or a chair. I mean, how many chairs has that man designed? I just couldn't dream of doing that. I don't know how he keeps doing it. Newson is a kind of diverse pop star, or he would like to think he is.

I had a weird dinner once with Verner Panton before he passed away, it was one of those moments that you stand back from and think, "oh my God, I'm having dinner with Verner Panton". Verner really did a lot with materials and a lot with plastics. I think he was more used *by* the manufacturers than used *to* manufacture, which is a shame because they used his flair and personality to produce some amazing work, but he didn't really make it. There is stuff like the Panton chair, which is a classic, but there is a massive body of work that just remained experimental pieces in the factory. Living Tower would be a great piece to have. Every time I see one at a show I think about buying one.

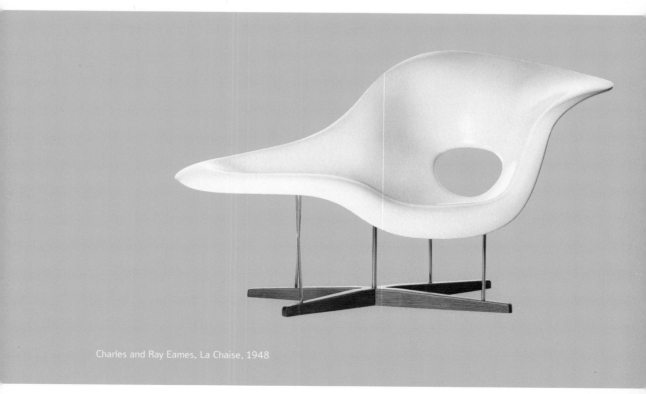

Charles and Ray Eames, La Chaise, 1948

Office in a Bucket, 2003

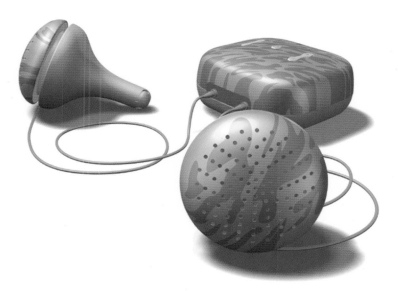

Plug and Play amp and speakers, 2003

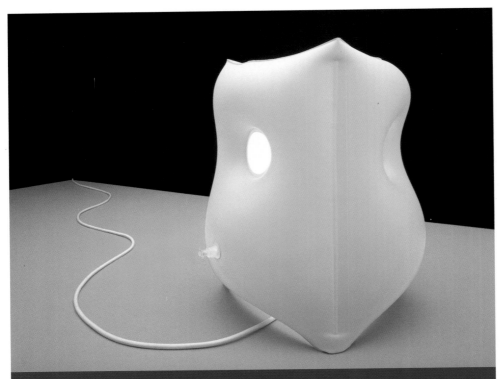

Table light, 1990

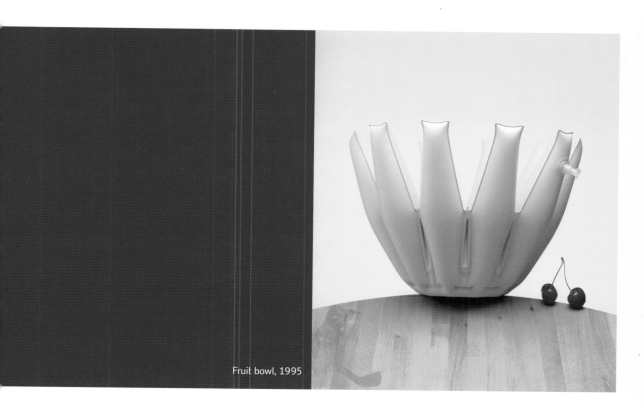

Fruit bowl, 1995

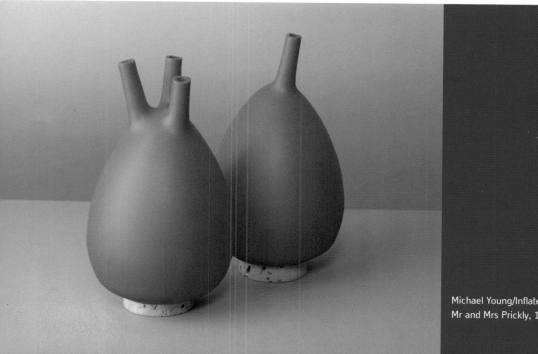

Michael Young/Inflate,
Mr and Mrs Prickly, 1997

I'm really bad with buildings because I never know the architects or the building names. I've seen tons of stuff recently by Rem Koolhaas, which is incredibly inspiring. His store for Prada in Milan is fantastic. It is exactly what architects should be doing — pushing the boundaries with materials and reinventing. When you build a building it's like a huge one-off, and the experience, all of this should be experimented with in just such a way.

Then there are buildings I like. For instance, the new London Assembly Building. The building is by, I think, Norman Foster. I love this building just because it's different, no other reason. I like its pleasing form and the fact that it's being done, whether it's intellectually correct or whatever, it's just the fact that it's not 'square' and it's in London and it got through planning permission.

I'm a big fan of Future Systems, of some of their earlier stuff, such as the Media Tower at Lord's Cricket Ground, in London. But I'm not sure about the stuff they are doing at the moment for Selfridge's. I don't know what is behind it. It's almost as if Selfridge's are buying into the image of what Future Systems was 30 years ago and they are just producing an image. The impression I get from some architect friends of mine is that it is not a very deep project. It's just what you see.

I also love the NatWest Tower. Hotels are also a favourite of mine. There are lots of hotels I would love to go and stay in. I would love to stay at the Hempel just for the hell of it. I've been to India and stayed in some amazing places there, some of them dilapidated, some culturally rich, and some left over from the colonial days. It's quite amazing to see the contrast between luxury and poverty. There are some buildings I'd love to go in. I tried to go into the NatWest Tower but failed. Apparently, you can book to go to the restaurant, but you would have to plan ahead....

Foster and Partners,
London Assembly Building,
1998-2002

I've got some Eames work, which I'm very proud of, some older pieces. A fibreglass DCM Eiffel Tower Base Chair. And there are other little bits and pieces, some of which have been given to me as gifts from students. They are not necessarily groundbreaking, but it is often more interesting to buy something off one of the students than buy something out of the shops. It's hard at the moment because I think there is a lull, with not much happening in the last couple of years. In saying that, however, I love the Droog doorbell with the two glasses, which is just a great little observation.

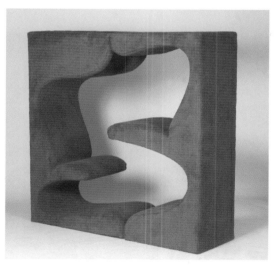 

Verner Panton, Pantower, 1968–1969

Peter Vander Jagt, Bottoms Up Doorbell, 1994

Charles Bukowski. *Women* is the classic one. You have to smoke and drink when you are reading it. Bukowski's books are all quite similar. They are all gritty. I've just read Naomi Klein's *No Logo*. That is one of the heaviest books I've read. I had to read it three times, reading a book in-between each time, because I had to read something more mellow. I was reading Tony Parsons's *About a Boy*. I read that in a day, but it took me five weeks to read *No Logo*.

Martin Pawley's *Terminal Architecture*. I haven't finished it, but I am really enjoying it and might re-read it. It's about architectural systems and questioning where things are heading, and what architecture is going to be, what it should be. Technology moves really fast, but architecture moves really slowly, and can it catch up? Can it plug-in and work with what is going in our lives? It's a good overview of how architecture has evolved and it provides a critique of the 'good' and the 'bad'. Like how London is just urban sprawl, it just keeps moving out, and out, and out. So, London is this decayed city, with wealthy new areas, old historical areas — which are wealthy, as well — and old areas with no content that more or less become ghettos. Pawley compares London with places like Hong Kong, where people couldn't move so they built upwards and, therefore, had to invest in architecture, really put money into it. This is a very different kind of expenditure to ours. In London we have spent on land and sacrificed community. But in Hong Kong they didn't have land — although, they've probably spent money and still sacrificed community.

Naomi Klein, No Logo,
book jacket, 2000

Charles Bukowski, Women,
book jacket, 1993

Lamborghini Miura P4005, 1969

cars

VW Beetle. I've got one at home. A 1966 was the oldest I could afford to buy at the time. When I was 17 my parents bought me an almost new Ford Fiesta and I didn't want it. I wanted a VW Beetle. I had the Fiesta for about seven months and I sold it and bought my Beetle, which has sat at home in my parents' garage for the last five years. It's a bit dilapidated but I can't sell it. So I'm waiting until I have enough money to have it professionally restored, which I know won't be an investment. I will lose money. But it's a goal in life — my aim to have the car restored to its correct state.

I like both the Lamborghini Arako and the Lamborghini Miura. It's the car that crashes in the opening scene of *The Italian Job*.

In the 1970s, the Mark I Ford Escort, it was a great car. If you really look at it, it is fantastic. If you look at Newson's new car, for me it's a Ford Escort. I'm sure he sat down, looked at that car and just 'Mark Newsoned' it. I do like a lot of the things he has done with the car. It's very interesting. I like the way the seat belts are done. It's good. I like how I can't buy it because it's a bit too much. There are details here I would love to have in my car. I would love to know if the tyres really work. It's a great project because Pirelli make the tyres for them. And, if you're Ford, you can get whatever the fuck you want. No one can just go to Pirelli and say, "Make me four tyres." To have that sort of client and be able to do that is just a dream.

The Audi A2 is a really interesting car. The way you can flip down the wheel at the front to put your oil and water in. That's a good honest approach to the fact that people can no longer maintain cars like they used to.

Nick Crosbie 95

Then there are really silly things like the Rover. What the hell is Rover doing? I can't believe someone can run an industry like that. It's appalling. They are not only ugly, they're just not special. There is nothing good about them. They are like a cross between a BMW and Rover, and anybody is more likely to buy a BMW.

It's not just the designers. It's the owners of these companies. They have to have a vision, and the problem in this country is that old, big industry doesn't have anybody who has the balls to put their head on the line, because it's all 'democratic'. So many interests run Rover now that you are not going to get a clear vision out of it. We were working for Smart for a while, and we got a cheque that was amazing, it went up to hundreds of millions — but not for us, of course. Swatch had to get out because the investment in making little plastic watches compared to making cars is a different world. I think it's a great car. I'm all for the fact that someone does it. We shouldn't knock people for doing something, even like the C5. People are so quick to put other people down, but if you don't do it yourself then you don't have the right to say jack shit.

> ... and the problem in this country is that old, big industry doesn't have anybody who has the balls to put their head on the line, because it's all 'democratic'.

Volkswagen Beetle, c. 1981

Nick Crosbie

The best film in the world is *Ferris Bueller's Day Off*. It's got the best line in it: "If you don't stop and look around once in a while, it might just pass you by." And that is just it, that is the type of philosophy I try to live my life by. Enjoy it, but sometimes stand back and take a look at it. Sometimes, in our studio, it is totally mental and I just stand back and look at everyone and think, "Fuck, what have you done?" That film just sticks in my mind. I have a pirate copy that I pirated myself years and years ago.

Sometimes I like trashy films. I try to watch films as much as I can but I watch a lot of videos now as we've a baby boy. Films like *A Clockwork Orange*, *2001: A Space Odyssey* and *Pulp Fiction*. I love their tone and I love the violence in *A Clockwork Orange* and *Pulp Fiction*. The whole film is nice and dark. *2001* has great sets.

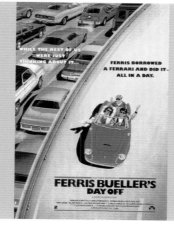

Stanley Kubrick, 2001: A Space Odyssey,
promotional postcard, 1968

John Hughes, Ferris Bueller's Day Off,
promotional postcard, 1986

I'm a really straightforward person. I really like Andy Warhol. When I was at college I went to a Pop Art show at the Tate and I got really into all of that. Bridget Riley, as well. There is an artist called Zoe Walker who does a lot of inflatable things that are quite interesting. Then you've got your Brit pop, like Damien Hirst, who is like Mark Newson in that he's also a brand name.

If you go to the National Gallery there are some amazing paintings. They are of great quality and just as inspirational as anything else. I think people forget about this work, as we see these paintings around as prints, and people have hijacked them for their own promotion. When you go to the NG and sit in front of an actual canvas it is stunning to think that is the original bit of kit. Damien Hirst works well on TV, magazines, and the Internet. You can buy into it, whereas with some of these other paintings, the only way you can buy into them is to see them for real. If you were to put a Hirst beside one of these works and ask which one had the most impact, I imagine people would find it hard to say that Hirst's work did. We tend to forget that. I sometimes have to force myself to go into these galleries, but when I'm there I find it really inspiring.

Nick Crosbie

I read loads. *The Guardian, The Observer, The Sunday Times*, and sometimes *The Independent*. But I don't read *The Times* other than on time apart from a Sunday. But if my partner goes out for the papers she buys *The Observer*. I won't buy two newspapers on a Sunday because they are all the same apart from the supplements.

I don't buy too many magazines, I used to buy *Arena*. I started buying *Arena* in 1986. The first cover I remember was John Paul Gaultier, and I remember a good article on Jasper Morrison. I didn't even know who he was then. It was funny because he used to have a studio upstairs from us and I once dug out my magazine and showed it to him.

My partner buys a lot of magazines, like *Elle Décor* and *Wallpaper,* so they turn up in our house a lot. I flick through them. I might read an article on someone I know, or if something was to catch my eye. I read the papers more. I'm really into the business pages. Business and sport. If I'm sitting in an office waiting for a meeting and there is a paper sitting there, then I think, "What do I have time to read? What will I read first, business or sport?" Business papers are good to read as you learn a lot of how businesses succeed or collapse. I read a lot about Marks & Spencer. I am obsessed with where that's going and have my own theory on how it might work. I like having theories on how businesses could be saved. M & S is suffering at the hands of brands like Gap, which have repositioned themselves as the young modern version of your basics. People always want basics, like T-shirts or whatever, and you want a certain quality. But the problem with Gap, and I used to buy a lot of Gap stuff, is that they stick big logos on everything. Now I don't buy any Gap stuff at all. And that's what M & S should do, make really good basics with no logos. Really good garments that are well cut — concentrate on the basics, and don't get all trendy. They are not a trendy store. And get rid of these big square lights that are all slatted. The shop is too big as well. They need to make it smaller. They're too much like supermarkets.

BMW, Air Camper, 2004

Motorola,
'Why Moto' campaign, 2004

100 Nick Crosbie

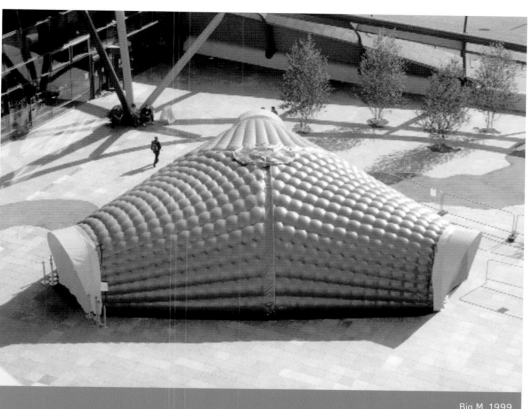
Big M, 1999

Pet Shop Boys all the way. Depeche Mode. I would have said Simple Minds, but only for their 1980s stuff. I don't like their recent stuff. I went off Simple Minds after their live album. Radiohead, U2. I get obsessed. You know, when you find a band you like and you buy every album. Loads of music. My partner buys music that she makes me listen to. Arty French stuff. I love 1980s stuff. I've got loads of 80s albums. Things like an album by someone called Felix. It had a green door on the cover. Good record.

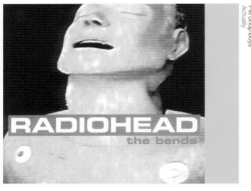

Pet Shop Boys
Actually

Radiohead, The Bends,
CD cover, 1994/1995

Pet Shop Boys, Actually,
CD cover, 2001

Nick Crosbie

people

Henry VIII — isn't he the one that had loads of wars, killing loads of people, taking over loads of countries? That's who I admire. I admire the get up and go attitude. William the Conqueror, people like that, they are the people, people who were prepared to put their money where their mouths were, to get together a big group of men and just go in and take what they wanted. Nowadays it is so frustrating. Sometimes I just think, "If only it was 1066, or whatever, then I would just get together a group of big chaps and just get what I wanted." It's all too complicated today.

I don't want to be like another designer. I can't think really — Bruce Willis. I don't think I'm like Bruce Willis though! If I were having famous people to dinner then I'd have to have Tony Blair, so I could have a chat with him about a few things. You'd want George W Bush there also, so you could lock him in the toilet and never let him out. If it were topical, then on principle, we'd have Bin Laden, Arafat and Sharon, and get them all around the table and say sort this fucking mess out. That would be great, saying, "Right, just sort it out, deal with it." There are loads and loads of people. I would definitely have the Eames'. There are loads. I could go on forever with that.

Henry VIII
Tony Blair
Yasser Arafat
George Bush

DUMoffice

DUMoffice was an Amsterdam-based design studio, founded in 1997 by Wiebe Boonstra, Martijn Hoogendijk, and Marc van Nederpelt. All three are graduates of the Design Academy in Eindhoven, The Netherlands. DUMoffice's particular approach to design was informed by their belief that each assignment requires a unique, intelligent approach to form and function, whilst emphasising flexibility. They combined novel materials, production techniques, and references ranging from sportswear to architecture.

DUMoffice's work has been widely published in Frame magazine, Interni, Surface, and the International Design Yearbook. Several of their designs have been exhibited at the Stedelijk Museum, Amsterdam, the San Francisco Museum of Modern Art, the Museum of Decorative Arts in Copenhagen, and London's Victoria and Albert Museum. DUMoffice's impressive client list includes Nike, Moooi, Abet Laminati, Belux, Frame and Stroom. The studio's main objective was to develop its product experiments into fully functional and commercially viable industrial products, either under its own name or in co-operation with manufacturers.

Recently, after seven years of intense co-operation, Marc van Nederpelt, Martijn Hoogendijk and Wiebe Boonstra decided to end DUMoffice. They have all now started solo careers.

Unkle Easy Chair, 2000

Martijn Hoogendijk: I knew at an early stage that I was interested in the field of design. I have been creative my whole life, really.

Wiebe Boonstra: We all liked drawing when we were little kids. For me, I was doing work experience as part of my technical education. It was at Philips, and there was this part of the office that was always closed. You couldn't get in because they were making lots of things. But one day I managed to get into that room and that room and this opened up a whole new world of design, which was when I realised I wanted to do industrial design.

Marc van Nederpelt: We all studied at a school dedicated to industrial design.

Martijn: You can do different things in many departments, but it is all under the same roof.

Marc: Almost like the Bauhaus.

Martijn: So, we would start with colour studies.

Marc: Ron Arad, he got a lot of attention there.

Wiebe: He's still quite fresh though, Ron Arad. No, that's a joke. But seriously, Martin Fischer, he's important to us.

Martijn: An old, Dutch designer who managed to make things look 'new', not like something from his time. His is an influence we got while at Eindhoven. Before that, I didn't know of many designers, only Pininfarina. And I don't know who we admired the most. There weren't so many. And not so much their work but their attitude. And there is also the fact that we were all at the same stage trying to discover the same things.

Wiebe: Like *Snowcrash*.

Martijn: It would be N2, if they still exist. If you come to find your own identity you can also see how other people are developing their own language and identity and that's what you see with Scandinavian designers a lot, especially the Finnish. Each time you are doing a project or making a product, it's the product or the context that decides what is going to be done.

Wiebe: I admire, not the ones who make a nice chair or a nice table or something like that, but those who go deeper in a certain area, such as Gaetano Pesce.

Martijn: Jean Prouvé.

Wiebe: Pesce's still making things in an area nobody works in. It's not commercial, it's not product. He works almost like an artist.

Marc: Pesce is very independent.

Martijn: Very confident in what he does.

Marc: Sottsass also.

Wiebe: Sottsass designs a chair, then he changes and changes it. He doesn't just design a chair and then the next week design another chair. He goes deeper into the one chair.

Martijn: I can admire someone for what he is doing, but think his work is totally shit. So, if you are asking if there are designers whose work I think is not important, then yeah, of course there are. Karim Rashid. You know the whole blobby style thing. I mean I am not against blobby, not at all. Perhaps I have never seen him work. More or less what we try to avoid ourselves is to have a branded style, like a formal language. Sure, I think every time you speak you use a language of form. That's the weak point of Newson right now. In the beginning he was really super-inventive.

Wiebe: It is very difficult because now he's being asked for this language with his products so he can't do other things anymore.

Marc: When your style becomes a trick then it's all over.

Wiebe: But in a way it's a good thing, although designers don't like it. The people who buy the stuff like it very much. If you were asked to design a wooden table and you design a wooden table, then the customer is happy. But if I were to give them a glass table, then they would not be so happy.

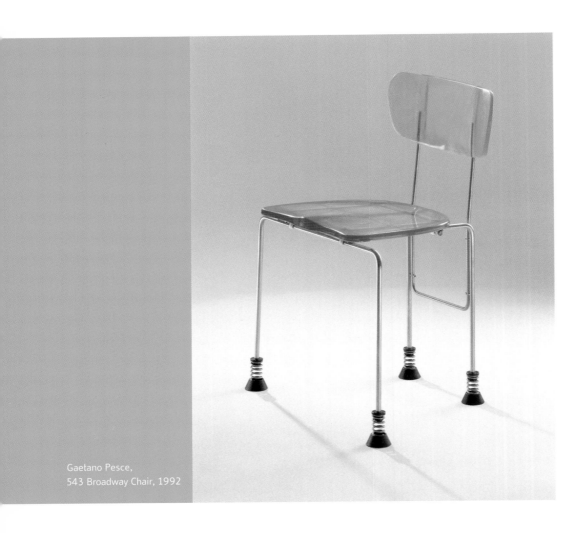

Gaetano Pesce,
543 Broadway Chair, 1992

I can admire someone for what he is doing, but think his work is totally shit. So, if you are asking if there are designers whose work that I think is not important, then yeah, of course there are.

Martijn: I think James Turrell's work is great at the moment. What you see there is someone who really understands how a space can be manipulated. So immaterial and yet becoming something too. Another one is John Maeda, doing anything with space. But that's computer generated design, starting from something more technical.

Wiebe: We have a fascination for concrete and glass windows, an experience of space. Like a club. Just a few walls don't play a role in the experience of being in a club. We're interested in height and music and other things.

Martijn: It's also the time. If you take film sets, for example, if you have enough time to look at everything close up, you think it's rubbish. But you see it for only a second. It's tricking your eyes.

Wiebe: Maybe not even a club, but where they do good parties, like in Rotterdam or Belgium, terrible spaces, dark and cold spaces. There was this one place with very loud music, but we liked it. There was only smoke in that space, and there were the strobe lights.

Martijn: Light, dark, light, dark.

Wiebe: It was a very James Turrell type space.

Marc: What is the club we went to in London?

Martijn: The Blue Note. That was fantastic.

Marc: A wall of sound.

Martijn: There was one part of it and we couldn't get in anywhere. And there was another part with nobody there and then when we opened the door we were hit with music. Wooomf!

Marc: The secrecy.

Wiebe: It was very hot. We found this cool area.

Martijn: The roof covered the whole stage. Yeah, it was like you were dancing, then you're wet immediately, and then it came over you like blow dryers.

Marc: The *Blade Runner* set, very intriguing.

Wiebe: Yeah, in Amsterdam there are people who really know things and have moved on. Only the people that don't have the urge stay there, with few exceptions. I would like to go from the south of Norway to the north, through the fjords. There are areas where it is totally grey around you.

Martijn: Go to the North Cap on midsummer's night, something like that.

Wiebe: Gran Canaria.

Marc: Japan, Brazil.

Martijn: Yeah, yeah, Japan.

Marc: The heritage of Amsterdam.

Wiebe: There are not many new buildings in Amsterdam on an architectural level.

Marc: It's a magnet for artists and the financial world.

Martijn: And scum.

Marc: For many centuries it was a place of trade and freedom, anarchy and liberal thoughts. The cultural centre is for tourists.

Martijn: It's not that different to Britain, I should say. Like London. Is it ten per cent of England's population that lives there?

Tokyo Streetscape, 2002

products

Marc: Once we were asked to name the best product ever and we came up with UPS. It's a total system, a global company. Nice colours, very practical. The efficiency, the tracking, and the barcodes all come together in this one happy world. It's an immaterial service. You can transport things from one world to another, but it's all totally squeezed into one image.

Wiebe: They don't change. A lot of companies change their logos to a more contemporary style, but UPS leave it their way. It's good.

Marc: Brown suit, brown shoes.

UPS Delivery Van

Wiebe: It's the one thing we hardly do, look at books about design because you only see things you know already, so it's more fashion and architecture. In art and fashion there are new developments, which we can learn about and use in our designs.

Martijn: I read the newspaper everyday. I'm a fact factory. I have a regular newspaper.

Wiebe: I started reading more about artists like Stephen Balkenhol and what he's doing. He makes wood sculptures. It becomes a lot more interesting with the background information taking away from the mystery.

Martijn: Sometimes, as a designer, you have to be political to get things done. It's all very much focused on the product. It's not so much about the bigger issue. You make a statement in your work and that's about the only level of politics we use. It really depends on the project you're working on. That's one thing I miss a little in the design scene. Maybe it's because it's not there and we shouldn't try to make something out of it. I think it's already dying. I think that in 20 years the biggest design studio will be Microsoft. I think anyone can pretend to be a graphic designer.

Marc: The environmental discussions don't exist anymore. Ten years ago everyone was talking about the environment.

Wiebe: It's taken for granted.

Martijn: I actually don't mind being superficial, but you have to get over it yourself. And I still haven't discovered what I miss in this field. We three have the same feeling sometimes. Like you think, "Christ! What is the bigger meaning behind a product?" But then you think, "Oh well, what the hell. I like it, it looks nice."

Sometimes, as a designer, you have to be political to get things done. It's all very much focused on the product. It's not so much about the bigger issue.

Premsela Design Foundation Office, 2003

Azam Optician Store, The Hague, 2002

Solar City Lounge, 100% Design, Rotterdam, 2003

or frame magazine | powered by de jager product, de ploeg, dumoffice, modular, toucan-t.

Baby Unkle Easy Chair for Kids, 2002

Martijn: Most of the ideas never see the light of day. Sometimes they really go out of their minds and that's what I like about it. Although I'm not so much interested in cars, I think the most beautiful car right now is the Saab 95, because it doesn't look like any other car. The transformation of cars is amazing. They can turn an ordinary car into a beast, like rally cars. Just by shaping the thing they can completely change it. So for me, that's the magic.

The transformation of cars is amazing. They can turn an ordinary car into a beast, like rally cars. Just by shaping the thing they can completely change it.

Rally car, Alex Milton, c. 2000

Martijn: There is not one kind of film. I like films with a 1970s atmosphere but shot five years ago. Some of the takes are so crisp and they look so natural. I also like a lot of films that were made in the 70s, like *Dirty Harry*. The surroundings were pure and natural, the fact that they weren't so concerned with the sets and environment. Now every movie is over-styled. It's not objective anymore. Like these big American films. When you see old movies, you think, "Wow! So much atmosphere." And then there's Ang Lee's *The Ice Storm*, because of its 70s atmosphere.

Wiebe: I like the really early movies.

Martijn: I like some westerns. That one with the really brilliant shooting. People are in this Mexican castle. *The Wild Bunch*. But I think the main influence on visuals is video clips. I think the main videos for me are the Björk videos. It's the ultimate expression in audio-visual. The four or five minutes that it takes is brilliant timing. It can be very authentic and original, even if it doesn't tell a story. A lot of visuals can be very inspirational to me. And I watch a lot of MTV.

Martijn: A big influence for us is Matthew Barney.

Wiebe: The video stills for his latest *Cremaster* look amazing.

Martijn: It's all about the mystery. I like to see what people do, but sometimes I'm not interested in why they do it because it takes the edge off it.

Martijn: I watch the National Geographic channel.

Sergio Leone, Once Upon a Time in the West, promotional postcard, 1968

Martijn: It varies a little. Electronic music. Basic General Label in Berlin.

Wiebe: Anything from the Warp label, especially the old stuff and, of course, the Detroit labels.

Martijn: I spent a holiday in Barcelona at the Sónar Festival. Music is, indirectly, a very big influence.

Wiebe: There's maybe 20 seconds a day here in the studio when there is no music.

Aphex Twin, Richard D James Album, CD cover, 1996

Stephen Fry
Freddie Mercury
Ian Hislop

people

Wiebe: People I would like to have dinner with would be the Queen. I think she gives a good state banquet.

Martijn: I want to have dinner with George Bush Junior. I want to know if he's really that dumb.

Marc: The first man, prehistoric man.

Martijn: J K Rowling, it's the ultimate success story. Better than Donald Trump.

Wiebe: I would like to have dinner with Tommy Cooper.

Martijn: If he can die on stage he must be really talented.

Wiebe: Freddie Mercury and Janis Joplin.

Martijn: That would be a very good combination.

Marc: Churchill.

Martijn: Yeah, because this sign has been explained as V for Victory, but here it means something else. The guy from the programme *Have I got News for You*, Ian Hislop. Also Louis Theroux.

Marc: Ruby Wax.

Martijn: Stephen Fry.

Marc: Oh yes, Stephen Fry, especially for his declaration of not having sex.

Mark Dytham / KDa

Klein Dytham architecture (KDa) was established in Tokyo by Astrid Klein and Mark Dytham in 1991. Having both studied architecture at the Royal College of Art in London they left for a three month tour of Japan to work for Japanese architect Toyo Ito. Today, KDa specialises in architecture, interiors and furniture design.

Taking the best from East and West, KDa aims to fuse different cultures effortlessly. The practice has no recipes, working with the client, programme and all the other parameters of the project to develop a unique, but above all, an appropriate solution that is fun and a pleasure to experience. Materials, colour, humour, and technology are all key elements of the work of KDa. Being based in Tokyo, with the Japanese thirst for newness ever present, their work is always fresh and challenging. KDa continuously searches for new approaches, which embody the moment — it is not afraid of now.

In 1993 KDa won the Kajima Space Design Award for best young architectural practice in Japan. Their building for Idee won both the Asahi Glass Design Award and the National Panasonic Design Award in 1996. In 1998 their interior for a new Information Centre at the British Council won a national award for best library. In 2000 *Architectural Review* awarded KDa Emerging Practice of the Year in their annual ar+d competition, which receives over 700 entries from 50 countries.

Leaf Chapel, Tokyo, 2004

Right now, I think, the guy we used to work for, the Japanese architect Toyo Ito, is a major inspiration to me. When I came over to Japan we thought his work was fairly interesting, but did not really understand it. And then we, that's Astrid and I, both ended up working in his office and realised that he was probably one of the most interesting architects in the world but nobody really knew who he was. There were only eight people in the office, and we made it up to ten. He's got this knack for looking at traditional Japanese culture and pulling different things out of it. Not in a literal way, but in a very soft way. He talks a lot about informality, and how events make architecture. So, when the cherry blossoms blossom, lots of people have parties under the trees, for like a week, and then the blossoms have gone and that event has gone. So, within, say, theatre, when there is an event on in the theatre, people congregate in the lobby and there is this kind of movement of people, and that influences the architecture. It is a very different way of looking at things than the way I was taught at university in the UK.

At college I was into the British designers, Norman Foster and all of those boys, like Nicholas Grimshaw. Generally, the boys who put things together very well. I wasn't looking at anybody who was dreamy or arty at that time. It was a very logical architecture that I was into then.

There is also a Japanese designer, Shiro Kuramata, who we met when we came over here. We were keen to work with Kuramata. I think he was quite a big influence to us both, but Ito definitely changed the way we looked at things. And Tadao Ando has been an influence. Currently, I guess we are looking at Rem Koolhaas' work, and a lot of other Dutch architects such as MVRDV. I don't know if we get inspired by these designers. I don't actually like looking at too many architecture magazines. We tend to get inspiration from other things. I don't get inspiration from architecture.

Mark Dytham / KDa

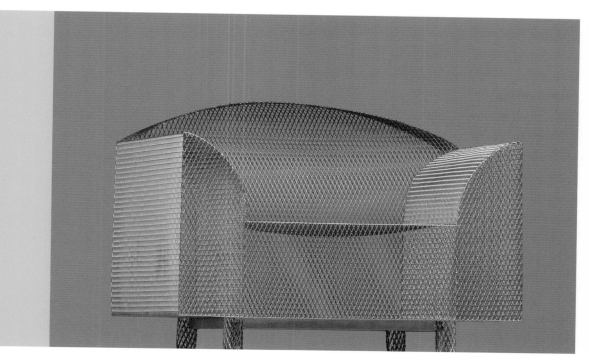

Shiro Kuramata, How High the Moon Chair, 1986

I don't actually like looking at too many architecture magazines. We tend to get inspiration from other things.

When I studied at Newcastle we were given an education, which was an engineering based education, and grew to admire the engineering works of Brunel. You know, I like cars and engines. I did metalwork at school. My dad worked at British Rail and made trains. He was a pattern maker, and my grandfather was a good woodworker, so there is this 'making' in my family. I came from that type of background where there was nothing to do with style or aesthetics. It was very much a practical education and the things I looked at, whether it was the Clifton Suspension Bridge, or whatever, the things that turned me on, were to do more with construction than art.

An important landmark for me is Milton Keynes. I go back there two, three times a year. You see this 'new town', which was built to a 1960s plan, and it has this flexible grid of roads on a one kilometre grid, and you see that grow over many years and it's not bad. Everybody knocks it and it is a joke, but it is bloody good. I have learnt a lot from that, putting in this very strong grid of something and then you spend the next 15 years trying to break it down. It is quite interesting and they kind of got it right I think, but nobody talks about it like that, it has this joke-like reputation.

And the shopping centre in Milton Keynes is one of the best in the world. It still rides above the commercial layer. It is somehow serene. It is like a temple to shopping, you know. Although, they have ruined it just recently, as they are building all this other crap around it, but the main building is absolutely phenomenal. That was important.

Obviously, Japan was a place I had to come to, especially Tokyo. I think that was because all the modernist architects came to Japan. And I am sure that is where the modernist aesthetic came from, from the shoji screens and the temples and stuff, very minimal architecture without any decoration. So, I wanted to come and see the real thing. Around 1988, when we arrived here, there was massive construction going on all over the place. They were doing these fantastic things, things you couldn't do anywhere else in the world. This was because there is no visual planning here, there is no review board and there is no fine arts commission. It was a pretty interesting place to come and see, especially at the time of the 'bubble', with all that money. So, I wanted to come and see both things. Other than that, I have not been to Brazil but I want to go to Brazil, and I definitely want to go to Mexico, because of the colour. And also India.

I think travel is really, really important. One of the things we say about our office is that we are not a Japanese office, and we are not a British office, we are a Tokyo office. I think that is quite important. We don't really care about the nationality. And by travelling you see differences. If you are always in London, you don't see London. If you are always in Tokyo, you don't see Tokyo. So, when I go back to London now, I see the chimneys,

Mark Dytham / KDa

because there are no chimneys here in Japan. And I notice the taxi drivers are completely different. I don't see the telegraph poles and all the electricity stuff in Japan anymore. It becomes normal, so it disappears from your mind. Equally, when I go back to London, I see this other type of visual pollution, which is worse I think, which is all the parked cars in the streets. When you come to Japan, all the cars have to be parked off the street especially in housing areas. It is kind of weird, but we can see things Japanese people can't see, and equally, we can start to see things British people cannot see. We are in this kind of inter-world and that's why I think travel is very important. And that is why we try and tell everybody, all our students, get going, go somewhere. It doesn't matter where you go. But go somewhere, it will help you see stuff in your own culture better.

Foster and Partners,
Hong Kong and Shanghai
Banking Corporation Headquarters,
1979-1986

Mark Dytham / KDa

Idee Workstation Furniture Showroom, 1996

Undercover Lab, 2001

Mark Dytham / KDa

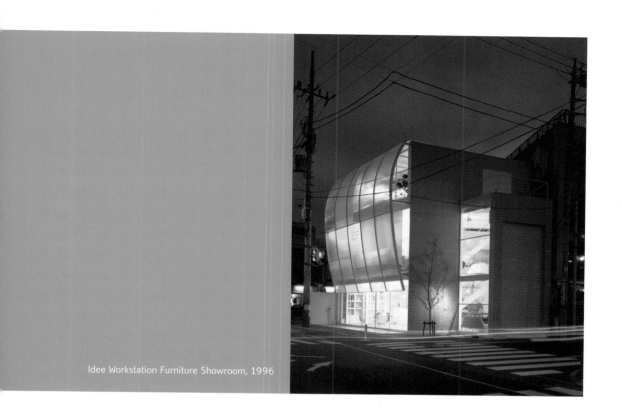

Idee Workstation Furniture Showroom, 1996

Beacon Advertising Agency, 2002

Mark Dytham / KDa

I just bought a Moulton bicycle, designed around 1962. But I bought it because it does not look like 1962. It looks like it's brand new. It's a design classic… and I've just written it off, but that's another story. I really like the designer Raymond Loewy, who did the Lucky Strike cigarette packet. He also designed the Shell logo. And the designer Dieter Rams, who does all the stuff for Braun. And Paul Rand. He did the IBM logo. Those sorts of guys, who are kind of pure. This is going off the topic a little bit, but I just love the Paul Rand story where IBM allegedly pays him two million dollars to come up with a logo for them and he arrives in the meeting, lifts up a board and says, "That's it! You either take it or leave it. If you buy it, it is two million dollars and if you leave it, it's two million."

I like products like the telephone jack. You know, the telephone 'plug'. Nobody really designed it, but it's such a universal thing that it's a classic. I mean, these products come into your life but nobody really knows who designed them. And products like the BIC pen, or the cassette tape. There are these things which I don't think anybody really looks at. It's that type of product that I kind of appreciate, as opposed to anything that has 'style'. They are anonymous products, but they are ubiquitous in terms of where they function. Car treads on tyres, they all look the same but where do they come from? That is what I regard as a classic, more so than a Philippe Starck Lemon Squeezer.

We always say that things around us inspire us. The normal inspires us. Everyday life inspires us. It doesn't have to be about art, literature or music. Inspiration comes from looking at everything in a close way. I went to an exhibition on the work of Paul Smith, and at the end it said, "If you can't find inspiration around you then you are not looking hard enough." That is what we say to our students here all the time. It is there, you have got to look for it. We are always looking at beer cans. We look at advertising, we look at all of that stuff. There is something in all of it — maybe the colours, it may be graphics, it could be anything. A hot air balloon. It's things around us, and that is where we get our inspiration. We get inspiration from the client, we get our inspiration from the problems we are given. The more problems the project's got, or the more difficult it is, will probably mean the better the project will be at the end of the day.

Lucky Strike cigarette pack,
Raymond Loewy, 1941

Mark Dytham / KDa

No, I don't read very much unfortunately. I read magazines a lot, but no books.

Aston Martin, c. 1960

Land Rover Range Rover, 2003

cars

I prefer to use taxis, I can make phone calls when I am in a taxi, I am relaxed, I can get prepared for the next meeting. I don't take the subway very much unless it is a long, long trip. I think I would say a Land Rover, the long wheel-based Defender, because I could get all the office in there, and the design has not changed in over 40 years. The same old rivet marks are on it, the same petrol cap and it is not really about style. I kind of like that whereas the Mercedes 4X4 Jeep has a bit too much style. When you have the Land Rover in your head, everything else sort of looks a bit overdone. Having said all that, as I used to live near Milton Keynes, I would love an Aston Martin one day, even if I only had it for six months. I have to have one just to say I had one. I like the classic Aston Martin DB. There is a certain something in the curve that is quite difficult to put your finger on, which is kind of nice. It seems fat and sort of full, it seems like it is full of engine and stuff.

I am a big plane freak. I actually fly a glider and I have gone solo a few times. But here it is really expensive to fly and it's a long way to go to fly a glider. It's a bit of a pain in the neck. I also windsurf. So, I like these forms of transport that don't take up any energy.

Mark Dytham / KDa

I think I come from a school that is a very British school, were cinema is kind of fun, it is not really art. That is how I was brought up and that is how it was at college, so cinema for me is entertainment. I find this Godard school of film a bit tedious, but I used to like some of his films at college. Obviously, people like Terry Gilliam, films like *Brazil* or *The Fifth Element* are really important to me. *Black Rain* is a pretty good portrayal of Japan. It is those types of movies that I kind of like. I haven't seen *Star Wars*, haven't seen *Batman*, did not see *Spiderman*. I would go and see *Austin Powers*, and I would go and watch *Being John Malkovich*. I don't like blockbuster films. I don't know, these films sit in this kind of funny, quite intelligent, and humorous at the same time genre. I travel a lot, so I see a lot of movies on the back of a seat. If you were to watch *Silence of the Lambs* in the cinema it would be fantastic, but on the back of a seat on a plane you're not scared at all.

I guess Ridley Scott is the key director for me. If I had to say a director, it's definitely Ridley Scott. *Black Rain*, *Thelma and Louise*, *Blade Runner*. It always rains in his movies.

I guess *Pulp Fiction* is a big favourite and I think my film collection tends to show where my interests lie. I've got all the Guy Ritchie films, *Lock, Stock and Two Smoking Barrels*, and I've just bought *Snatch*. I love a lot of Monty Python stuff, that just does not date. I mean you can see *Life of Brian* today and none of those jokes date for some reason. I don't know what it is. It's kind of slapstick but it's pretty pure.

Monty Python,
Life of Brian,
promotional postcard, 1979

Quentin Tarantino,
Pulp Fiction,
promotional postcard, 1994

Mark Dytham / KDa

artists

Artists like Alexander Calder and Picasso began to switch me on to art. Today, I don't think there is anyone I would say we go to and use their work for inspiration. We like a lot of contemporary artists, and I am trying to think of one desperately right now. I have forgotten his name, I will think of it in a moment. He is a guy who will cut a hole in a gallery floor and it will be perfectly cut, and it will be dug down and it will be sprayed out with matt black paint. So you think that it is square on the floor, black, someone has put black paper on the floor — Anish Kapoor! Some of his installations are totally bizarre.

press

I read magazines like *Wired* and *Wallpaper*. I read magazines a lot. I will read *Wired* from front to back cover, whereas I tend to look at *Wallpaper* and read some of it. I read a lot of stuff on the Internet, which soaks up all my reading time. The *Wired* site has this really cool site of links to other news sites, and these tend to be mainly scientific. I read *The Economist*, for its current affairs and technical current affairs. It's this I'm most interested in. I probably buy a newspaper once a week, *The Japan Times*, which I buy on a Wednesday.

Museum Cafe, Tokyo, 2003

Leaf Chapel, Tokyo, 2004

Mark Dytham / KDa

Bloomberg ICE, 2002

Pika Pika Pretzel
Temporary Hoarding, 1999

Mark Dytham / KDa

This tends to be British influences again. It is a bit like the cinema. I am not into full-blown pop and I am not into classical either. I am sitting in this Elvis Costello, Aphex Twin kind of area. You know Pet Shop Boys would be the limit of pop for me. I should get my iPod out and have a look and see what I have on there at the moment. But it is the clever lyrics that I like — Dire Straits. I listen to the lyrics quite a lot, and I liked the cleverness in Billy Bragg's music when I was at university. Music helps me when I am tired and I can't really find the energy for the next couple of hours, so you put your headphones on and it takes you somewhere else for a bit and it becomes enjoyable again to work. It's really important first thing in the morning when I get up and it is pretty full on in the morning. It is pretty loud music. It is not soft, classical. I can see my taste is changing. I am becoming a bit more grown up.

Aphex Twin, drukqs,
CD cover, 2001

Billy Bragg, william bloke,
CD cover, 1996

Mark Dytham / KDa

That is a difficult question. There are all kinds of inventors. So, it would be somebody like Alan Turing. Again, this all comes from where I grew up in the UK. Bletchley Park is in Milton Keynes and that is where, in some way, the computer came from. It never dawned on me as to the importance of who this guy was, and then you find more and more about how he worked, and the incredible pressure the guy was under to produce results, to break codes and stuff. And people like Clive Sinclair, individuals that really go against the grain and have a vision. His vision, of course, was that everybody would have a computer in their house and when he brought out the ZX80 or whatever it was called, everyone was saying, why would you want one of those in your house? But he had this vision that everybody will need a computer, and today nearly everybody in the Western world has a computer. He also made the first digital watch, the first digital calculator. Those types of people are kind of important.

I think the spirit of people like Richard Branson, people who mix business with pleasure and are entrepreneurial in a kind of non-aggressive way like, say, Bill Gates are also significant to me. I would not mention Bill Gates as a person I want to aspire to be. But I see what Branson does as a kind of interesting way forward, rightly or wrongly. I do tend to identify with the entrepreneurial spirit. People like Steve Jobs. Again, more of a computer geek, but that guy has an invincible vision. He will not let go. We are big Macintosh freaks, obviously, here at KDa. But I admire the way that his philosophy is taken all the way through, especially in the new software they have brought out. I mean, it is incredible that this guy has turned the company around. It's hard to believe that somebody can go back in after the company went completely, sort of, haywire and lost its direction, and turn round four to five thousand people, and change the face of computing again with the iMac or the iPod, and whatever else they have produced recently. He has this incredibly clear view of a very complicated situation. And he goes against the grain. He might only have five per cent of the market, but he helps produce things that everybody says are the best things in the world.

I know Jonathan Ive, the chief designer at Apple, and I think, to be fair, the two are very good together. On their own, Jonathan without Steve, it would not have worked because I think there is a clarity with what Steve Jobs does that I don't think happens with Jonathan. Jonathan excels when they are together, I think he gets the energy from Steve Jobs. I think that's fair, I don't think anybody does anything on their own, it's always part of a team effort. What I found recently with Apple, is the combination of the software and hardware, the new software is as well designed as the product is. The way it all integrates, they got the picture, they understand where this whole thing is going and you really need someone to overview it like they've done. Whereas Microsoft is going off with all these security problems. And so Apple are the sort of people I would like to work with.

Mark Dytham / KDa

In terms of dinner party guests, there would have to be more than one as we find the more people round the table, the better it is. Who would I choose to come to dinner? You would have to have a Pope there. It would not really matter which one, but there would be a few things to sort out there. Mother Theresa would be another person I would want to invite. And an American president from around the Cold War, possibly John F Kennedy. I think Kennedy would be important, just to see how close we really were to all out war at that time. And I think I would invite, although I said I don't really admire him, Winston Churchill, just to see if he lived up to his myth. Lastly, Leonardo da Vinci, probably, someone like that if you are going way back. That's a weird bunch.

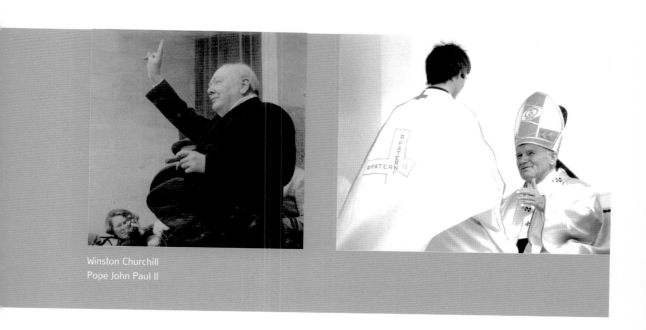

Winston Churchill
Pope John Paul II

Martí Guixé

Martí Guixé was born in Barcelona in 1964. He studied interior design there, and then industrial design at Milan Polytechnic. After working as a design consultant in Seoul during the mid-1990s, he began a long collaboration with Camper, the Spanish shoe retailer, in 1998. He has designed Camper stores all over the world developing a distinctive design for each one within the same visual language of anarchic illustrations and anti-materialistic slogans on its packaging, such as "If you don't need it, don't buy it", on Camper's bags.

He is committed to designing "brilliantly simple ideas of a curious seriousness". Martí Guixé spends one third of his time in Barcelona, one third in Berlin, and the other third travelling. Dubbing himself an "ex-designer", his anarchic humour is reflected in his rolls of sticky tape printed with images of an ornate picture frame or of footballs — so that the tape can be rolled up to form a ball, to the Key Brush he designed for Die Imaginäre Manufaktur, in Berlin, with the bristles dangling from the shape of a key.

As a "product designer who hates objects" Martí Guixé is something of a conundrum. He reconciles himself to his professional role of continuing to develop new products because "I need to use them" and by focusing on the functionality of his designs, rather than what they look like and the materials they are made from.

Galeria H2O Chair, 1998.

Actually, I do not have much interest in design. I agree that there are nice, or interesting, ideas in the world of design past and present, but I cannot mention one figure. I strongly separate the work and the person. There are very interesting designers whose work is really boring and vice versa. I admire people who think and deal with ideas, any kind of people, not only designers. I don't believe in inspiration. Design is an intellectual process based on acquiring and processing information mixed with politics. Yeah, of course, there are designers who have influenced me. My design studies were during the 1980s, which was a total Memphis time. The designers working as part of the Memphis group heavily influenced everything for me around this time. Then, about the time I was graduating, in 1984 or 1985, I think, my influences moved towards the Ulm School in Germany. Ulm were refusing all these avant-garde styles and pushing the old school values from Germany. So, actually, I don't know, I was really a little bit between these two design influences. Nowadays, I don't follow the design world. Of course, I know what is going on, but I don't follow it much because I feel I am far too busy. I prefer to follow the art world. I find the art world more interesting as it is more about ideas, and design is mostly about shapes. So, I could not say that there are any specific big name designers who influence me — I don't know.

Actually, I do not have so much interest in design... I prefer to follow the art world. I find the art world more interesting as it is more about ideas, and design is mostly about shapes.

Martí Guixé

Ettore Sottsass, Teodora Chair, 1986-1987

Martí Guixé

I don't know. For the work I do with Camper, I think the biggest influence are the people who work Camper, like the chief designer and the owner. They have a set way of thinking, but they don't influence the result in the shops, for example, the Camper shops that use graffiti. I don't know if you have seen the Camper shop in Notting Hill, London, but it all comes from the situation. Camper initially asked me to do a temporary shop, to make it very 'easy', using materials that can be thrown away afterwards. So, in this situation, with their brief and the philosophy of the company, I made this kind of shop using graffiti. Camper always want people that express opinions, so with the shoeboxes it is more the environment that determines a result. The influence here is from the architectural world, or other scenarios.

I am very interested in everyday life. For me, the most interesting thing to see is how normal people are living. For example, if I go to Milan and I am staying in the house of someone I don't know, for me the most interesting thing is to see what they have at home and how they arrange their normal, everyday life. Mostly, I like dealing with people's lives more than doing pieces in my 'designs'. When I was in Tokyo I was more interested in observing how people deal with their normal daily lives — how they eat, how they work. I was less interested in what the buildings looked like. So, that is why when I am travelling, I try to approach normal situations, to be in normal restaurants, to see how people are proceeding with their day to day lives.

I admire very much the small, temporary, amateur buildings that people build for themselves, usually using different precedents. In Germany, for example, there are a number of areas where people have a small weekend house. These small houses are called "Lauben". This is very interesting as people build these small houses in their free-time, and they have a small garden, but they don't have electricity, and they don't have water. And they go there on Sunday, or just to relax. They are all over Germany, and they are like self-construction, very amateur, and that is interesting as it is a kind of architecture, popular architecture and it says a lot about the people. I admire this type of architecture a lot. In Spain there are these small, amateur, self-constructed bar-restaurants on the beach called "Chiringitos". They are built in a very provisional way. They do not have a toilet but are very close to the sea water.

Here in Barcelona it is becoming more and more like Canada, you know, very generic, very wealthy and very clean. Before the Olympics there were a lot of temporary constructions on the beach — they were mainly restaurants. They had no room for dining, only the kitchen, and you were eating on the beach, so you knew if it was raining the restaurant would be closed because they could not put the tables on the beach. I liked this idea, that the building is only for the kitchen and you eat in the open space. And, of course, it was illegal, so when the Olympics came they cleaned away a lot of these constructions because they did not have sanitary conditions for restaurants. I think if you go to the south of Spain you can still find this type of building.

I also admire the socialist architecture of the former East Germany, such as the Plattenbau in Berlin.

Plattenbau, Berlin, c. 1950

Martí Guixé

Stories, more than products, inspire me. I like the story about how the ancient Japanese dealt with a plague on rice plants. They organised a party where they caught all the insects, and then they ate them with rice wine. This activity is similar to the paint parties in Germany, where a party is organised to help to paint someone's apartment. I also like the story from Spain about tattooed virgins, or Spanish prisoners, who have a tattoo on their back to avoid punishment. This says a lot about the functionality of tattoos, which I love, and is one of the reasons I worked with functional tattoos. Stories on food, on parties, on everyday situations give me more inspiration than objects. Only objects that tell a story are interesting.

There are classics. There are things that I like very much but have not bought, and things that I did not like but bought because they work. It is difficult to say now, but sometimes a designer makes something interesting and you think, "Ah, it's good. It is not for me, but it's good." And then other things, which are very functional and you buy them because they are well done, but really not interesting as design pieces. I am trying to live very generically, so that is why I like generic pieces, but they are not interesting as design pieces. And, then, there are products like Playstation or the PC. I don't like how they are designed, but they are very functional. You do not choose a computer by the design, you choose it for its characteristics, weight, or its dimensions. Sometimes, I miss this — that the pieces are less designed when usually I think they are over-designed, in terms of their shape.

I don't like exclusive design, the idea of exclusive design pieces. And, now, there is this kind of retro-fashion exclusive! I think it is too, you know, too exclusive. I don't like this idea of designing something to be exclusive. The problem for me is that I do things very cheaply, like the tapes, for example. But what happens is, I cannot reach supermarkets, as the system is different, and so this work goes into exclusive design shops, like Colette, in Paris, or Moss, in New York. But, then, because the piece is very cheap, these shops don't like it. They prefer to sell very elegant and expensive pieces that are, probably, very trendy at the moment. So, what happens is, I am in this place where there is difficulty in doing this kind of design as there is no possibility of distributing it to most people. That, I think, is a big problem. Now what people understand as design is only what is exclusively distributed through design shops. There is a gap between, say, the 'cheap' chairs by Jasper Morrison and the white plastic chairs you find in every supermarket. So, the best idea, I think, would be to find Jasper Morrison chairs, very cheap, in the supermarket. Why does this not happen?

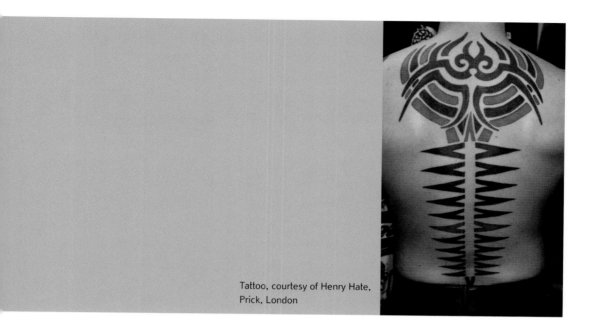

Tattoo, courtesy of Henry Hate,
Prick, London

Stories, more than products, inspire me. I like
the story about how the ancient Japanese killed a
plague on rice plants. They organised a party
where they caught all the insects, and then they
ate them with rice wine.

PVC isn't too well considered. In fact, its poor reputation began shortly after it first appeared in 1931. It initially seemed to be a clean and friendly invention, a chemical derivation of chlorine and petroleum that would eventually make its way into our lives. Now PVC is a victim of the same arguments that it once used to do away with its main competitors in the construction sector, asbestos fibre and uralite, substances accused of causing similar problems to those that now have condemned PVC. So the idea is to replace it with other materials that do not lead to the serious toxic effects that this composite has for health and the environment.

J.B.

PVC Bath Curtain, 2002

Home Aprons, 2001

Martí Guixé

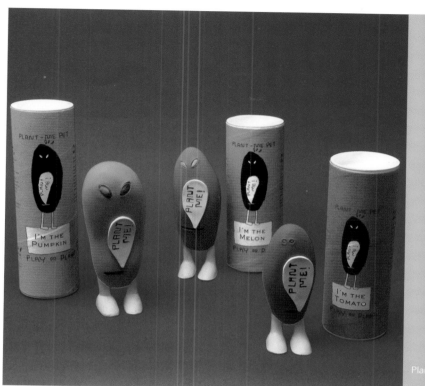

Plant Me Pet, 2003

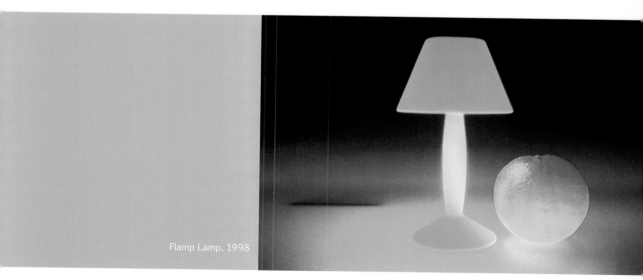

Flamp Lamp, 1998

I am continuously reading, and this depends on what I am developing. So, reading helps me a lot in my work, as it gives me a lot of information. For example, when I was doing the Los Angeles Camper shop I was reading books by a sociologist and architect from Los Angeles who writes about LA as a political and sociological situation. It is very interesting. Usually, I don't read novels. I like the story of the universe in *A Brief History of Time* by Stephen Hawking. Yeah, and I am very fascinated by genetics and biotechnology and science, so I try to read these things. But it is sometimes difficult for me to understand them. That is why I appreciate Hawking. He wrote in an easily understandable way.

And, of course, I search for a lot of information on the Internet. I go very deep into very concrete things. For example, I wanted to use an orthodontic system and material for some models, so I read a lot about this orthodontic system — how dentists do things with teeth, the processes and the way they use models to show their clients their own mouths. That is what interests me, to go very deep into a specific situation. At the moment, I am reading a lot about what happens, politically, with multi-nationals. I also used to read a lot of science fiction, most notably Bruce Sterling.

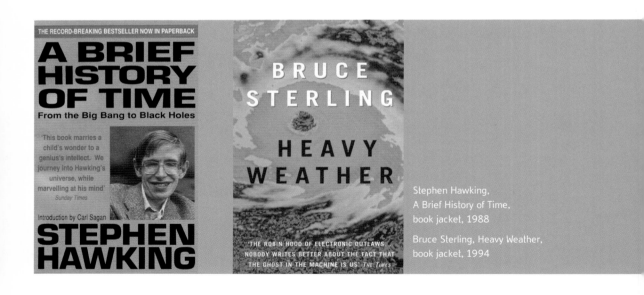

Stephen Hawking,
A Brief History of Time,
book jacket, 1988

Bruce Sterling, Heavy Weather,
book jacket, 1994

Tokyo Taxi, 2002

cars

I don't admire any car. I use cars, but I am not interested in them. Any kind of transportation is very uncomfortable. For me, the best form of transportation is walking and the Internet. I spend my life between Barcelona and Berlin. Well, actually, it is one third here in Barcelona, one third in Berlin and the other third I travel. I try to travel less, but it's not always possible. I mean, if you work for companies abroad you sometimes have to visit them. But I would prefer not to. I would much prefer to work through the Internet. I mean this Barcelona-Berlin thing, I don't see as travel because I am moving there for long periods of time, one, two months, maybe three months in one place. But going to a place for two days, I prefer to avoid that.

Nowadays, the most pragmatic and intelligent way of transportation is through drugs, TV, alcohol or religion, where your mind is elsewhere but your body is not moving. Transporting your body is something romantic when you do it for pleasure. Or something you have to do for work, but don't want to. When I was in Japan recently I saw very funny cars. I liked them a lot. They were very square cars. I think they might have been taxis — small private cars for transportation, very square. But no, I am not really very interested in cars. I know that is a very important subject in design because there are these transportation design issues. But actually, I bought a car two years ago, and it is not very difficult to find a car that fits.

cinema

Actually it is about three years since I last went to the cinema. I find it very boring compared to the written stories. I prefer video art, looking at sequences. They don't tell stories. They are more about ideas. It is very difficult for me to remember the names, but there are people doing interesting things. I like Chris Marker's *La Jetée*, which Terry Gilliam based his film *Twelve Monkeys* on. Chris Marker's film, I don't know, was from the 1940s. Ah no, 1962! It is a very interesting film because someone is travelling in time, but not in a machine — which was the trend at the time — but through some drug. So, for me, it is a very visionary film — this idea of biotechnology or drugs. I like Jim Jarmusch's films. I also admire Abel Ferrara's films generally, but especially *New Rose Hotel*, based on a novel by William Gibson. In general, I find it difficult to like film, which is why I go to the cinema less and less.

Martí Guixé

I like Thomas Demand quite a lot, because he is presenting this kind of clean generic world. His works are a little bit like images from the era of socialist states. For Demand, however, it is the approach, which is completely different as I read his work. Also, I like Thomas Hirschhorn a lot. Hirschhorn is a Swiss artist who makes things with scotch tape and materials like that. He makes sculptural displays and installations by combining very trashy, banal materials. I feel more interested in this artist's work than, say, in furniture design, for example. Generally speaking I don't like plastic artists. I don't like painting. I prefer installation or conceptual art. I know there are also some, as you say, old masters, who are very interesting, but not for me. I also admire a lot of the new British artists. In particular, the artist who worked with his own blood — Marc Quinn. I think, for me, he is more interesting than Damien Hirst, for example. I don't know why, but in general, they are communicating too directly.

Thomas Hirschhorn, Unfinished Walls, 2004

I always read the local newspaper. I read a lot of newspapers here in Barcelona and when I am in Germany. I am fascinated by catalogues, from product catalogues to supermarket catalogues, anything that shows a range of products — anything. I don't collect these catalogues, but I try to get them through the car industry, like where you can buy optional extras for your car. These catalogues are huge in Germany. Big catalogues with hundreds of things that you can buy. And furniture catalogues, and electronic catalogues, because I like to see how they arrange sets of products. Mostly, they are more interested in design and systems than single objects.

Only electronic music. Pole and Thomas Brinkmann are my favourites. Pole make something like dark electronic music and Thomas Brinkmann makes more, like, dry techno music — very, very German. They are both German. So, German electronic music I like a lot. I did an exhibition recently and I met Scanner, he is also very, very good. I listen to music on the Internet. I have several CDs by these people, but I like when they are doing more than just music. I listen to music whilst working, and when I am searching for music I search for electronic music which has some concept behind it. I remember three years ago, during the summer here in Barcelona, I heard a group from Canada called The User. They did music with old computer printers where they were programming some sentences in the computer and then 'printing' it using microphones, and you were hearing these sounds. It was really fantastic. I am very interested in this kind of conceptual music.

Martí Guixé

I am not interested in the idealisation of some historical figure. When I went to Germany I was really very interested in this system that socialism was trying to develop in former East Germany, because it was a very designed social system. And, of course, it is still a very interesting topic. I cannot say that I feel close to any figure in politics or design. I am now designing a kitchen for someone, which is a reference to Charles and Ray Eames. OK, it is a kind of homage, but it doesn't really mean that I am close to the Eames'. It is like they are interesting, but they are designers from the USA and, well, they did this kitchen and now I am doing a kitchen, which is a reference — but I cannot give you the parameters.

I am always looking for people, to connect ambitious people with projects. You know, it is very difficult to find people who want to develop a project. Okay, I am a designer and I always need somebody to put this or that idea into production and distribution. And this is a very important person and when you find interesting people, for example, the owner of Camper, then very interesting and commercially successful projects can develop. It is really hard work to find these people. So, if I were to invite people for dinner I would invite those — people, but I don't know who they are. I don't know who else I would invite, perhaps the Queen of England, I don't know. I am trying to think who I could be fascinated by. It is not that I don't like people, but I don't have anyone in mind.

Queen Elizabeth II

Thomas Heatherwick

Thomas Heatherwick is often described as a 'true' multi-disciplinary designer. The Thomas Heatherwick Studio, founded in 1994, was set up to combine the skills of architecture, public art, design and engineering. With a growing reputation for inventive and original solutions and a genuinely diverse team, the Studio takes a practical and hands-on approach to the application of artistic thinking, working on architecture, infrastructure, exhibition design and installation projects.

The Studio's work is rooted in research and experimentation. Fascinated by materials they take a collaborative approach to problem solving. Whatever the scale of the project, from the smallest product to large buildings, the same attention is given to detail and the development of ideas in the workshop.

The philosophy of the Studio is the desire to keep testing and experimenting with different genres, not to sit back and repeat past successes. For the future, the Studio has expressed a desire to be involved in the design of different building types, such as inexpensive housing and the construction of power stations — areas not noted for design. By not siting themselves firmly in the art, design or architecture professions, they have created a multi-disciplinary practice suggesting a model for future design.

Plank Folding Coffee Table, 2001

I actually don't want to answer that one. That is one of those questions, and I usually don't say that at all, but I don't want to answer that one. It is certainly a question that gets asked quite a lot, and I just don't want to answer. I have never given that response before. But quite seriously, it's a question that has a very revealing answer and that is why people ask it straight up. I have a standard answer, but I am bored by that answer, and it is the answer I would feel that I needed to give you or a very direct one that would be too direct.

People always answer, "Oh, there is not one person. Lots of things, bits and pieces of lots of people influence me." I don't want to give that answer as it is boring, and I don't want to give a little hit list of people, like ingredients or flavours. The only thing I would say, and here we go, is that there is one designer who has influenced me, for the energy, and for the way, as much as for their design, for the method, their method of achieving what they have achieved.

You know, some people have a kind of good idea of their lifestyle, that kind of thing. I would like to be a bit like them. The designer that influences me is someone who I was interested in primarily for his or her lifestyle. I wasn't put off, whereas I find a lot of designers put me off. That is the answer to that question. I bet everyone else has kind of come up with a nice little list of about four, five, six designers. It is because when I have read answers to that, I am a bit bored by the answer. I didn't want to give that answer.

Hate Seat, 1996

Thomas Heatherwick

I can't answer this question either, as it relates to the designer question. Architecture, generally, is my interest now more than ever because I have become quite bored of small scale design. There are just so many people doing it. And I am interested in the gaps that exist to do new things rather than doing my version of what other people are doing. I am quite 'un-stimulated' when many other designers are working in a similar field. And, so, I am interested in 'fields' more than I am in 'design'. Architecture seems to be a field within which there are many fields that have not been successful yet.

Buildings, environments and spaces — there aren't many things that are as stimulating and interesting, and well-functioning. All these beautiful things can be found in the world of architecture. There are thousands of artists doing art who are trying to achieve certain things, and thousands of young furniture designers trying to do their furniture… and product designers trying to come up with the latest gizmo, and great advertising minds coming up with cunning, clever advertising campaigns. But what excites me is when people find a new area within which to do their thing. Santiago Calatrava discovered bridges that weren't there before. There was actually a gap, with great things possible within the area of bridge design — that was exciting for me. Then, a lot of people come along and they want to do a bridge too. But I think, for me, it's those breakthroughs, when somebody suddenly spots that something could do with another lease of life, and there is, again, an area that can be revitalised. I think furniture was really interesting in the 1950s, 60s, and 70s, with new materials being pulled into design. Like, what do you do with plastic? And what do you do with this foam? And I love that, because then there is a real push, there is a material and an immediate connection. Whereas now there is someone designing something that the designers of the 1950s were playing with. Unless you are really pushing it forward, go home! So, I have set standards that might be too high for myself. And there are so many people trying to go for it. I feel that there are quite a few saturated areas of design, and so I am quite interested in the areas that are neglected.

I think there is a lot more room in these areas. And it is definitely architecture that interests me. It's here that you find people having kind of had original thoughts of how to do things. And that's the challenge, not to just follow the things you presume you know. Architecture is the ultimate discipline. It is so complex. It's got so many pressures — time frames and other things to consider. I think it is quite extraordinary. And good architects do not make presumptions. Recently, I went to a talk by Daniel Libeskind. And it was quite shocking how few people were present at the exhibition venue he was speaking at, which was a main event here in London. It was quite last-minute, but all the same I was there thinking what a funny thing, how underrated

Thomas Heatherwick

architecture is. If this had been a popular music event Libeskind would have had four minders. And whether you like him or not, he is doing some really interesting work at the moment. There were not that many people in the room, there were empty seats. I really like Libeskind's plans for the Victoria and Albert extension in London. I don't know if it is finally going ahead or not now. There is a new Director at the museum and they want to do it... all of the delays are just about money.

Another interesting building is Kungstradgarden Station. In Stockholm, theatre designers, artists and architects have been commissioned to work on the underground. Unlike in London, where the tube has been burrowed through mud and earth, in Stockholm it is blasted through rock. In Kungstradgarden Station, they have left the rocky walls intact and rough. They have taken the condition of being underground and really worked with it. The walls are mossy and the platforms are placed clear of the craggy wall so that water dribbles down the wall behind you as you wait for your train. It is lit dramatically, and in one place the walkway pulls away to reveal a collection of old sculptures. In other places the walls, though still left rough and contoured, have been plastered over, then coloured and patterned. When I first saw it, I was shocked — I couldn't believe I hadn't heard about this before. It blew away my prejudices about the Swedes being the ultimate arbiters of minimalism. Kungstradgarden Station is passionate, enthusiastic, raw design.

Thomas Heatherwick

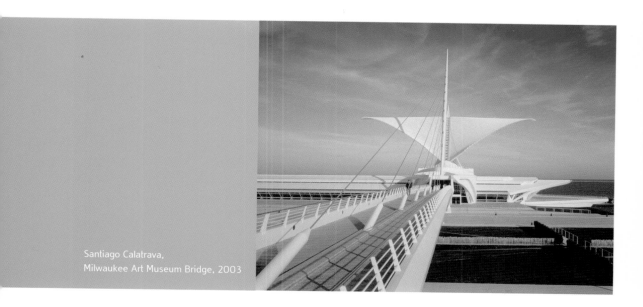

Santiago Calatrava,
Milwaukee Art Museum Bridge, 2003

Daniel Libeskind,
Jewish Museum Extension to the Berlin Museum, 1998

Harvey Nichols Autumn Intrusion,
London, 1997

Japanese Temple,
Kagoshima, 2004

Blue Carpet, Newcastle, 2001

You want a product? I can give you a number of them. I will tell you the kind of things I really admire. I would love to meet the person who invented the Pyramid Tea Bag. I don't drink tea by the way, but I think it was a good idea and it was an innovation in a non-design world. Someone was applying themselves to something that was a kind of closed, dead market. I am actually all clued up for this question because I have been asked to be a collector for products, at the Design Museum. I have to buy their collection for the year, and I have been thinking about it and really feeling quite repulsed at the idea of buying furniture that I like, and realised the things that I enjoy are original ideas, little original ideas. It's not necessarily the ones that I think are highly valued, but rather those that give me a lot of pleasure. I have actually got one that is slightly ridiculous. I went to Pizza Express recently and asked for a pizza and was given the most ridiculous bag. Someone has invented a pizza bag that is a plastic bag, like a napkin, with these little corners. You place your pizza in it and the corners stick out, and you can carry a pizza with the corners sticking out of the side, and it holds the pizza level. I just love the idea, that someone had that idea, someone went to Pizza Express and someone said, "Yeah, let's do it." The product is called "Sack Rock", I think, and they've got their patents and everything. Things like that, I find them very interesting and as stimulating as when you design a watch or something like that, even more so.

I think, though I have yet to eat one, that Pop Tarts are a good invention. Innovations in food, the idea of using a toaster to 'make' food rather than toast. I used to get a toaster and put it on its side and get pitta bread and put jam in, put it in sideways and push the thing down. I have never tried Pop Tarts — apparently they are really disgusting. And they come with a massive caution as they can burn your mouth. But I like the notion that someone came in to Kellogg's and said, "I have a great idea", and took it to market. I am interested in inventions more than in designs. That is what really stimulates me. When I was little I wanted to be an inventor. But I found out there are no inventing courses. I could draw and had quite a 3-D mind, which ended up taking me down a design route. I sort of mutated that route into a more architectural one. But the thing that stimulates me is innovation, the invention, original ideas, and that, I think, is whatI really enjoying seeing.

Thomas Heatherwick

I am interested in inventions more than in designs. That is what really stimulates me. When I was little I wanted to be an inventor.

Pyramid Tea Bag

Pop Tarts, packaging, 2004

I don't get much time to read these days. I would say that no book has really influenced me. Books kind of work in that you can refer to them to bounce yourself against, but I have never read one book that has really changed my direction.

What car has inspired me? I have admired many different cars, there's not one car in particular. I've had a Citröen 2CV for 11 years now. It's kind of the studio's van, my home car and my personal transport. It is everything rolled into one. I admire my old 2CV for this. I find it funny when everyone laughs at it. I find it interesting what it says about perception, how something is perceived. I really like how the 2CV looks, how it works and how simple it is to use. It does not have water-cooling or any fancy things. It's certainly as simple as you can get a car nowadays, and spare parts cost £20 rather than £400. A car is, in a way, immoral. I am a bit against cars, really. A piece of furniture you can arguably say, "I don't really want to get this dented as it is a beautiful piece of furniture" and, therefore, it stays static. But the idea that you don't expect a car, when it is moving around a city — as most people tend to live in and around cities — to get bashed and dented is crazy. I am not a bad driver. I am not an ambitious driver. I just drive quite solidly. I don't pride myself on my driving. I just find it funny that there are these cars that are a disproportionately high value for the risk they face, and then people are furious when something happens to their car.

I don't know a lot about the car world, but what interests me is the people who innovate within the industry. Citröen. I feel there was a time when Citröen was innovative. Citröen interests me as it innovated with its suspension systems, the way the car worked, and they produced beautiful, innovative models, like the Citröen DS. But I would not be seen dead driving a Citröen DS, as they are so pretentious. Otherwise, I think they are wonderful. I think it was Ron Arad who once said, and it really stuck in my mind as I thought it was a brilliant thing to say, "You don't have to own it to consume it. You can consume it without having this pressure to own it. Why do you have to own it?" These comments were in response to someone who was saying, "I can't buy these chairs as they are £14,000 each and that's ridiculous." I thought that was a good one.

Thomas Heatherwick

I would not be seen dead driving
a Citröen DS, as they are so pretentious.
Otherwise, I think they are wonderful.

Citröen 2CV, c. 1960

Citröen DS, c. 1955

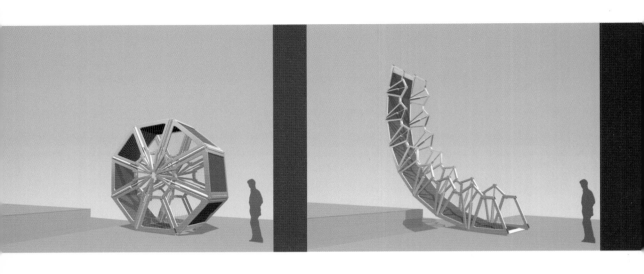

B of the Bang Sculpture, Manchester, 2004

Thomas Heatherwick

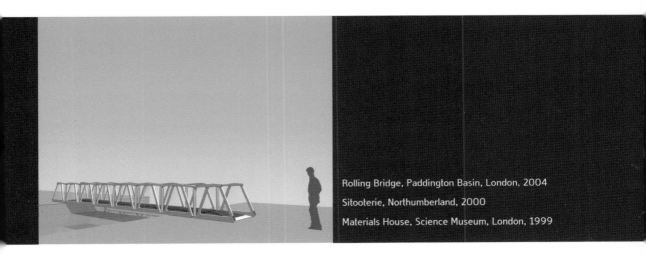

Rolling Bridge, Paddington Basin, London, 2004

Sitooterie, Northumberland, 2000

Materials House, Science Museum, London, 1999

I studied film at one point, as a sort of supplementary thing. And the person who we spent a lot of time on was Alfred Hitchcock. What interested me with him was how inventive he was with little things. He developed new ways to use the camera, and new ways to structure film. He was playing, really playing with the whole subject rather than just what he was going to film and what the story was, and I think that completeness is fantastic. He was also very clever in that film was an area that had not, for the most part, had that done to it before. Hitchcock came in at the right time, whereas now I bet all the young filmmakers are saying, "I want to be the next Hitchcock." There was something with his movies that had that inventiveness. Now when you look at most modern films, Hitchcock has already done it — he has made that one big step and unless you can really do a different kind of thing, it doesn't work. I think people forget that. They want, in a way, to follow Philippe Starck, for example. I bet every product designer says that they actually want to be the Philippe Starck of the modern world or something totally different. Hitchcock, on the other hand, made an area out of an area that did not really have something there. And he has now made that. So you cannot, you cannot have a bit of that. You can only do your own little version. If you really want to be Hitchcock, you need to do what he did in a different way.

I particularly like one Hitchcock movie, called *Rope*. I like this film not so much for the film, but because he, allegedly, did the whole film in one take. This is a truly brilliant idea. Apparently, when they were making the movie everyone had to learn their lines for the entire film. Then there is the other Hitchcock classic, *Vertigo*, where he perfected the technique of running the camera, moving the camera in closer to someone while at the same time zooming back using the camera lens. This suddenly gives you a very nauseous feeling. And this is now used regularly in adverts. But it is that dichotomy that I like. An engineer I know has an aeroplane, a Tiger Moth, and I stupidly asked him a question, as there was one bit of steering at the front with which you could steer to the right and a bit at the back as well. So I said, "What would happen if you steered to the right with the front and left with the back?" And, in a way, that's what Hitchcock did with the camera. He is pulling back while zooming in, it's kind of going left at the same time as going right. The plane started doing this and I started feeling sick, so I kind of had my lesson. But that, that really contradictory thing is what I love. It's not one whole film *per se*, but it's more the little bits — the idea that I really admire.

Thomas Heatherwick

... Alfred Hitchcock. What interested me with him was how inventive he was with little things.

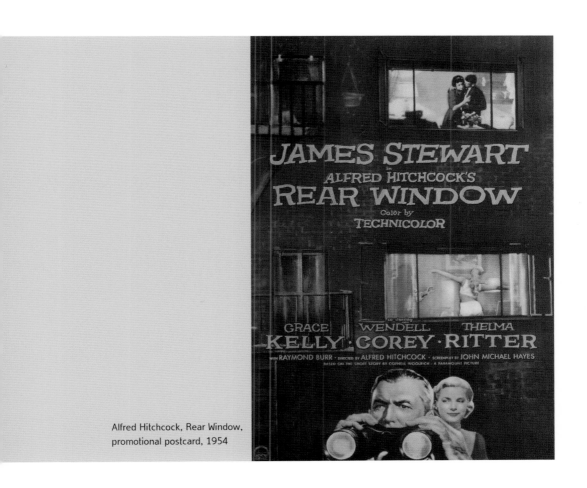

Alfred Hitchcock, Rear Window, promotional postcard, 1954

Thomas Heatherwick

I don't separate art from other creative arenas. I don't like the word artist. I don't like the definition. I really don't like the separation. I have to sometimes be called an 'artist' and that makes me cringe. Because when someone is really good at something, they say he is an artist. And you think there is a whole profession of people who are called artists. You know, when someone is a really good architect they get called an artist — only if they are really good. But anyone can call himself or herself an artist. I see it as all one area really.

I don't like the word artist. I don't like the definition. I really don't like the separation. I have to sometimes be called an artist and that makes me cringe.

Thomas Heatherwick

press

I don't read newspapers. In terms of magazines, we get mainly architecture magazines, such as *Architectural Review*, *Architects' Journal*, *Blueprint* and things like that. But we also get *Plastics and Rubber Weekly*. We don't subscribe to magazines like *Form* or *Domus*, but luckily we have had articles on our work in different issues. We get foreign things, but you just can't subscribe to 30 different journals, and I don't feel I have to look at them.

music

I have been listening to a lot of Elvis Costello recently, he is someone who has innovated in his work. He plays music that is familiar, but there is something different about it. But I don't like his voice that much, as I find it irritating. I don't really listen to music that much.

Same as the first answer. I can't answer that. I have been very interested in people like Brunel and I was also very interested in Buckminster Fuller. But these two individuals are not revealing the person you want me to. I think Brunel was living in an amazing time. I admire someone like Brunel because his ideas were not just great ideas. I think people always mistake someone like Brunel as just having had great ideas, but it is the whole thing about running a company that people overlook. His company was delivering ideas and delivering infrastructure. I mean, it was for a reason. It was for railways. It's having a reason for inventing that I think is interesting. Even though I enjoy looking at innovation for pretty reasons first, like tea bags and things, they are kind of steps forward, but this does not mean that I want to define my life in such a way. Someone like Brunel must have been really great, he must have been really stimulating. But I don't know if you would call him a designer or an inventor. People love to call people things.

I recently got to know Ron Arad. He has made efforts to be friendly to me, and has invited me to things and got me involved.... And I think he is someone who is quite fascinating. I admire a huge amount of his work for the way he kind of combines a whole lot of ingredients and looks at things three-dimensionally. A lot of people sort of innovate in quite two-dimensional ways, but I think he thinks very three-dimensionally. The objects that he has designed are really three-dimensional. Your eye enjoys looking around them and that is something that I have been really interested in. We try to do this with the projects we are doing, both objects and spaces, in that they are not just an idea. I don't like the word sculptural, but there is so much architecture that is not very good for the eye. We try to design things that have a number of complex relationships to them.

I develop all my ideas with 3-D scale models, and with chat. We kind of verbally do things. I might do some exploratory drawings, but the emphasis is always on the 3-D model. For me, modelling is my drawing technique, and so we make all these models. I don't trust anything unless it's three-dimensional. It's funny because making models has become quite fashionable again. Daniel Libeskind, who people think of as this great theoretical architect, wants people to know he makes models. At Libeskind's talk, he mentioned that he had been reading books on Frank Gehry and how Gehry makes loads of models, and how he currently makes a lot of models in his own work.

Thomas Heatherwick

The thing is, lots of people say I innovate, I am very innovative, and I push boundaries. I think people don't realise how many boundaries there are to push and I think Arad pushes many boundaries. He has pushed the boundaries of materials, form, scale and a whole lot of things. These are things I have a common interest in, so it has been great for me to get to know him more. I don't know if we will work together. At some point it could be possible, but I don't know.

I develop all my ideas with 3-D scale models, and with chat. We kind of verbally do things.

Buckminster Fuller

Thomas Heatherwick

Scott Henderson

Scott Henderson studied at the University of the Arts, graduating in 1988 with a degree in Industrial Design. After graduation, Scott worked for a variety of design firms designing everything from furniture to lighting to aircraft interiors. Scott joined Smart Design in November of 1993 where he is currently Director of Industrial Design.

Scott is known for is ability to transform the mundane, believing that if something makes you smile it becomes easier to use. Scott's design work for some of the largest corporations in America has generated numerous awards and media attention. Henderson's work has been included in ID Magazine's Annual Design Review seven times and has received four Gold and two Silver IDEA Awards, five Chicago Athenaeum Good Design Awards, two awards for Excellence in Universal Design from the National Endowment of the Arts, as well as a 2004 Medical Design Excellence Award. He is listed as the inventor on over 50 United States and European patents.

His work is in the permanent collections of the Smithsonian's Cooper-Hewitt National Design Museum and the Chicago Athenaeum. Henderson has lectured on design, both nationally and internationally, and has published many articles on the importance of design in periodicals such as *Inovation*, the quarterly journal of the Industrial Designer's Society of America and Design Management Institute's *Design Management Journal*.

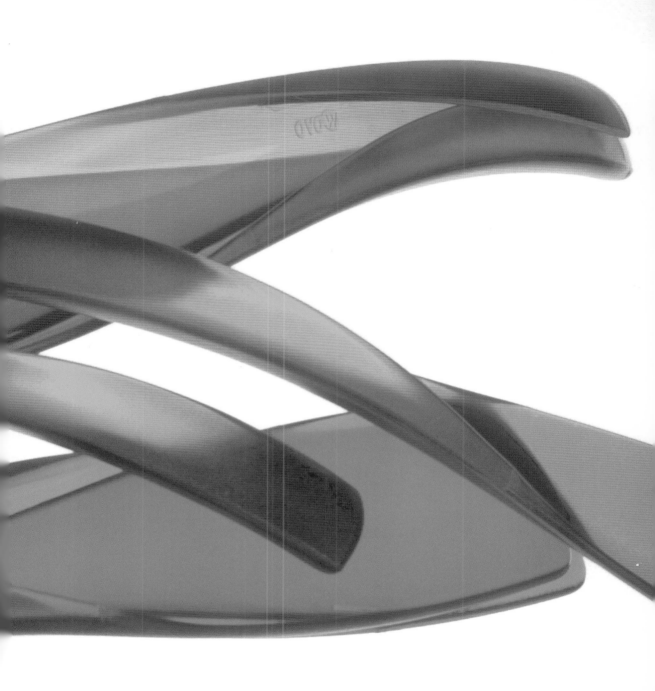

Wovo Salad Servers, 2001

Well, I guess from the past it would be this designer Pierre Paulin, a French guy from the 1960s or 70s. He did some really cool chairs and things that I thought were inspiring because they were sort of three-dimensional. I guess when you boil it down I'm kind of a sculptor, you know, and I'm trying to use industrial design as a medium because it's fun to have one of your sculptures mass produced 200,000 times over. But, I mean, my *forte* — there are a lot of designers out there with different *fortes* — my thing is form and sculpture also realising things three-dimensionally. I couldn't do without being creative, working and making things. I get a charge out of completing something, starting something and finishing it. Or doing something that will trigger a reaction from a huge cross-section of people. It is inspiring when I get a reaction, not from many words but just seeing that I can make them smile. That's a real rush.

There's another designer, Serge Mouille. I think he's French, maybe Belgian or something. He's another amazing guy. He did a lot of lamps that were really beautiful, made out of single sheets of metal bent into these beautiful shapes. It's amazing what you can do with just a single flat sheet of metal. They are the two great designers from the past, and then there are the usual suspects, like Charles and Ray Eames. I'm doing a chair right now that I'm trying to make out of plywood. It's the subtle beauty of the forms that are so simple yet really complex, you know, when you really study them. And, then, modern, I guess I was really inspired by Philippe Starck. He is an icon. It relates to something I have written down here about mirrors and looking backwards. He seems to have this ability to do that. It's like he's in a parallel universe. He comes up with these things that seem so obvious, but not until you see them. It's like a little commentary on the way we perceive things. Like everything you see in a mirror seems exactly familiar, but actually it's exactly the opposite. You don't pick up on that because it's so subtle. So, that is what's interesting about Starck — that you can do something that seems very familiar, but in a subtle way, it's very twisted and the reverse of what you might expect. Whenever this is present in a design that I'm doing, or someone else has done, I feel like there's a breakthrough, and that's interesting. And there's also the thing about mirrors. Not literally, but like the reflection of what's happening in life... as it's applied to design it's a very abstract kind of thing, it's hard to put into words. A big part of successful design, in my opinion, is almost cultural commentary. They're like three-dimensional brainteasers or statements about our preconceptions, or the way we're supposed to see things.

Scott Henderson

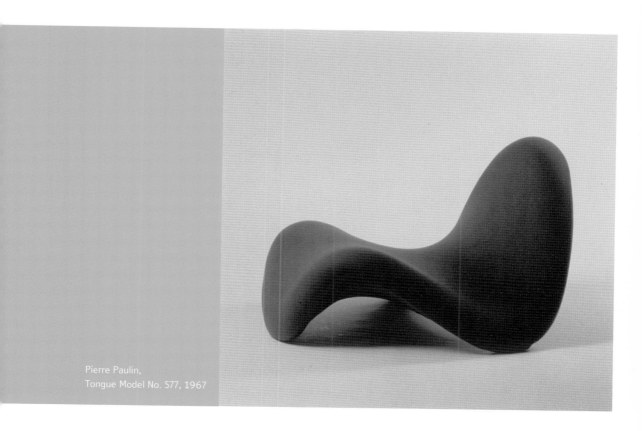

Pierre Paulin,
Tongue Model No. 577, 1967

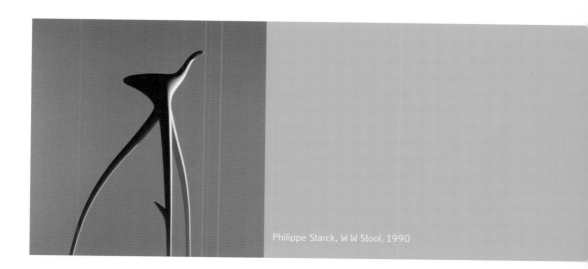

Philippe Starck, W W Stool, 1990

Scott Henderson 179

Charles and Ray Eames, LCW (Lounge Chair Wood), 1945

WOVO Chip and Dip, 2001

WOVO Ice Bucket, 2001

WOVO bowl, 2001

Scott Henderson

OXO suction cup soap dish, 2001

That's a good question. I always thought that the AT&T building here in Manhattan was great because it was kind of ballsy to put this sort of Chippendale dresser up as a building. It's by Philip Johnson. I mean, there's something about that that I always thought was kind of cool to be able to get away with. The stuff that he did in his early career — the glass house. He's actually done so much. I just think it's cool, like in a lot of corporate product design you have to go through so much focus testing just to get a blender produced, or to get a toothbrush made. Focus test it galore, spend a million dollars on just the focus testing and here you can throw up the Chippendale dresser, that affects our skyline and is something that will be there for 100 years, or whatever, and, you know, it's a whim. It's something right off the top of his head. There's something really great about that. And it's another commentary, like I was saying before about really good design having some sort of commentary on culture. It's kind of like Pop Art. It's like saying, "Why can't a can of soup be art?"

Scott Henderson

That's hard. I liked Philippe Starck's Juicy Salif when it first came out, even though everybody thinks it doesn't work and it's bad design. A lot of people think it's good design too. I thought it's a great example of taking an approach that's less expected. I don't have one though. I don't really collect stuff like that. Just stuff from the flea market, but I still admire it.

Philippe Starck,
Juicy Salif Lemon Squeezer, 1990

Scott Henderson

Uh, lately I've just been looking through design related material. But I remember reading *The Fountainhead* by Ayn Rand. I was pretty inspired by the passion going on and the two approaches taken by Howard Roark and Peter Keating — the one guy really trying to push the envelope and change conventions and the other guy who is working under these conventions. Yeah, that was amazing. It was also sort of design related because it's about a struggle to change the world through signs.

THE FOUNTAIN-HEAD AYN RAND
THE WORLDWIDE BESTSELLER

Ayn Rand, The Fountainhead, book jacket, 1943

Scott Henderson

I like the Porsche 911. It's beautiful and well resolved. It looks friendly and powerful, it's passively fierce. It's not screaming macho or anything — yet it is. It's an incredible car and it hasn't changed much. It's become an icon. It has not changed dramatically since the early models, which were also incredibly cool. And now, as its body has stopped changing, it just sort of evolves, which shows how classic and perfect it is. And I was thinking of an analogy. Something I like in design, that makes a good design, is contrast. So, the car analogy would be like Maserati and Citröen when they did a car together as a joint venture a while ago. When you look at that car it seems like the wheel base is in the back because it's narrower in the back, and maybe it is, but that's unexpected. You might think it should be even, or the other way around, and because there's that kind of contrast the car is inherently kind of interesting. There's something about contrast that makes things interesting. It shows up everywhere, like in movies, like a spy movie that has some beautiful blonde who is a weapons inspector *and* a lethal weapon. That kind of contrast is interesting. If a design has that level of contrast it's sure to be pretty interesting.

I like the Porsche 911. It's beautiful and well resolved. It looks friendly and powerful, it's passively fierce. It's not screaming macho or anything — yet it is. It's an incredible car and it hasn't changed much. It's become an icon.

Maserati Gran Sport, 2004

Porche 911 Turbo, 2004

The movie *Chinatown* with Jack Nicholson, because it's sticking to the whole detective genre, and because there's a real dark side to it. I like the fact that they use certain genres like Asian culture as dark and mysterious and evil. And I always liked *Brazil,* because it shows technology and bureaucracy running amok.

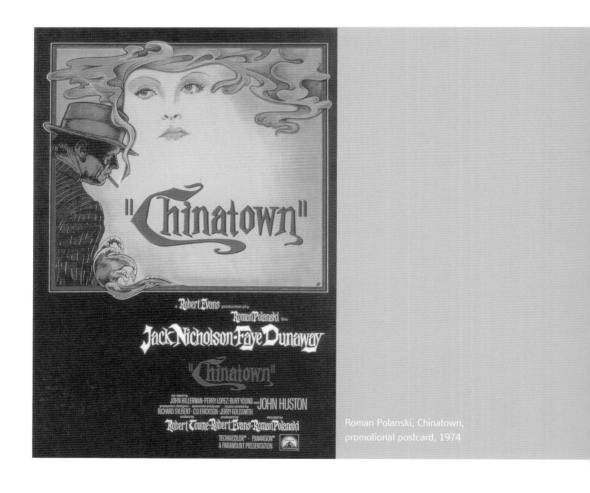

Roman Polanski, Chinatown, promotional postcard, 1974

Scott Henderson

Brancusi's stuff is good. Another one would be Alexander Calder. I went to his show a while ago and I was really blown away by how prolific he was and how it seemed like he had this stream of consciousness ability to create. He would be able to go into an exhibition that was going to open the next day, I think he had done this, and he would show up with nothing except for a big spool of wire and some clippers and he'd create the work right there the following day. There's something extremely powerful about this ability that I really admire. It shows that he is immersed in it, there's a total immersion, you know, his craft is his life, and he's able to turn out something of quality that has an identifiable character that we recognise as his own — that's incredible. That's the mark of someone who is a good designer, that they have this creativity and it's not that they're born with it. It's taken over their lives and it's become second nature to them, like eating. It's the people that are doing it nine to five — part-time designers even though it's a full-time career — who are less prolific and struggle more.

Scott Henderson

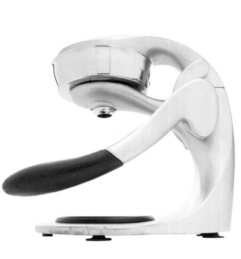

WOVO thermal carafe, 2001

OrangeX Ojex juicer, 2000

XM SkyFi Satellite Radio, 2002

Scott Henderson

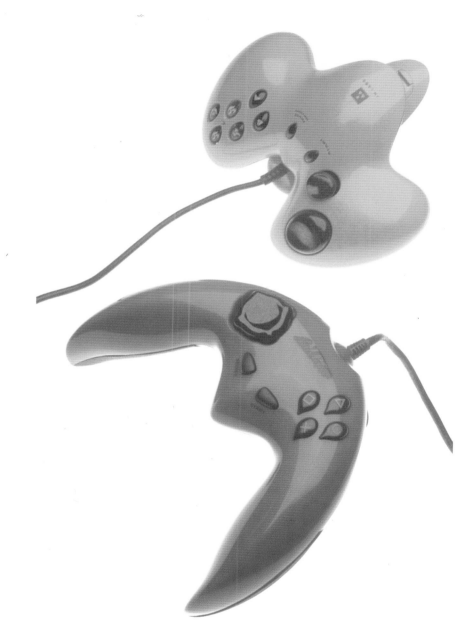

Alps Game Controller, 1997

I read *The New York Times* and *The Post*. *Wallpaper* is great. I think it's an amazing magazine. It's remarkable that they can put that out every month. And *One* magazine, which is a new sort of American version of *Wallpaper*, it's also pretty good. And another one called *Surface* is great for design. Some home furnishing magazines are kind of interesting like the Italian *Casa Grazie*. And *Wired* is sometimes interesting. They're good for seeing what people are doing with material and form and sometime just the way something is photographed, it evokes a point of view. So, that's good for keeping current with stuff like that, and it's inspiring.

Recently, I've been listening to some techno, head-banging stuff, like the Prodigy. It jars you, sort of clears your head. Marilyn Manson has this great tune, I can't remember what it's called. And Rage Against the Machine, I mean, those aren't my favourite bands or anything. Things like the Chemical Brothers. It reflects what I want to do in breaking into new territory. Putting your headphones on and cranking it up — it's like freshness.

The Chemical Brothers,
Dig Your Own Hole,
CD cover, 1997

Rage Against the Machine,
CD cover, 1992

Scott Henderson

Let's see. Maybe John Lennon. There's something about the sort of music John Lennon and Paul McCartney did that is so amazing, to have that level of consistency across so much work, the way that it evolved.

Maybe also Joe Torre, the New York Yankees manager. He seems like a good, upstanding guy, and a good leader. That's impressive when somebody has the ability to do that. If I could invite anyone over to dinner then it would have to be Alexander Calder.

There's something about the sort of music John Lennon and Paul McCartney did that is so amazing, to have that level of consistency across so much work....

Ichiro Iwasaki

Ichiro Iwasaki was born in Tokyo, Japan. He commenced his design career at the Sony design centre in Tokyo in 1986 where he carried out various development projects in car audio systems and TVs for the European market. In 1991 he left SONY and moved to Milan, Italy where he worked as a product designer. In 1995 Iwasaki returned to Japan and established the IWASAKI DESIGN STUDIO. He designed and produced the MUTECH brand product line in 1999 and since then has become a Design Director at the company.

His design work encompasses general product design, including household goods. Currently he is involved in the design of an array of products, from tableware to home electronics to information tools, such as mobile phones and digital cameras.

Iwasaki's product designs have recently been featured in, amongst other publications, the *International Design Yearbook*.

Mutech Music Centre (prototype), 2000

There aren't really any specific designers that I admire. For example, if you asked me what brand of clothing I like, I don't follow a brand. I don't search for the 'label' of a particular T-shirt. I don't look at a designer and think that good things always come from that same designer. I look at each item they do in turn, and I like certain things — but I also dislike certain things. So, it isn't really important which brand or designer I like. It is the item I look at. And, there are so many good things on the market, that it is very hard to say, "This is a good thing." For example, if a person listens to classical music, and only likes classical music, they can be a bore, because things aren't like that. There is good classical music, but there is perfectly good popular music as well.

When I was a student I had an interest in product design, but information on other designers was really limited at that time in Japan. I thought Mario Bellini was fantastic. I was particularly impressed by his work for BrionWega. Achille Castiglioni and Vico Magistretti were also both heroes of mine at this time. There are so many approaches to design, and often it becomes a matter of whether you like it or you don't. In terms of design approaches that I don't like, I do not like the work of Luigi Collani. I do not like the point that he is really stuck on. His style — morph-like form. Everything he does is so twisted. It is very hard for me to admire such a designer. He could be an experimental designer, but he is stuck in his way and does not explore other things. It is very hard for me to be influenced by a designer like Collani. In my opinion, Karim Rashid also falls under this umbrella... there is a similarity between them. They both seem to be stuck with organic forms. But Rashid is not at the level Collani is.

I think Alessi is, simply, great. I like Alessi because I think they try things more than a company like Sony. If you work like Sony you have to think about how to promote products, and you have to sell a certain amount of product. So you could say that Sony's approach to design is really limited. In a company like Alessi, of course they mass-produce their products as well, but they are more free in their minds, they're interested in more than just mass-production for profit. So, I think Alessi, and companies like them, stand out. Although Alessi hire a lot of designers for their product ranges, I don't have one designer in mind that works on Alessi products. I couldn't do that. Again, it is very hard for me to specify a designer, because I may like certain items by them, but not others by the same person. If I were to mention a designer I would mention someone who was where I wanted to be when I was at their age.

Ichiro Iwasaki

Mario Bellini,
Cab Chair Model No 412, 1976

Stefano Giovannoni, Lilliput,
Salt and Pepper Set, 1993

Stefano Giovannoni,
Merdolino Toilet Brush, 1993

Ichiro Iwasaki

Again, this is a very difficult question to answer, but something that just popped into my mind is the graveyard in Milan. I think it is called Monumentali in Milan. I like graveyards generally for their 'total' expression. My visit to Milan was the first time that I had gone to a foreign country. I was 19 years of age and I travelled around Europe. When I look back at that time, at my visit to Monumentali, it was really outstanding because it was totally different from what I thought of as a graveyard. When you think of a graveyard in Japan, there are usually tombs. Even in America there are crosses standing on the hill, but when I went to Monumentali it was a place of expression. There are things there like sculptures and glass façades. It looked like an entrance to a clothes boutique, but all made of glass. And the glass wasn't clear, but slightly tinted — it wasn't frosted glass, but transparent. For me, this was a lot about what the building represented. It was a graveyard, of course, but it was so beautiful, it was more like a boutique. As I was only 19 at the time, so death, and the graveyard, were really distant concepts for me. But I felt was that Monumentali changed my concept of what a graveyard should be. It was really outstanding.

I have an architectural project going on right now. I go to Kyoto about twice a month at the moment. I don't really like a specific building or design, but I do like the overall cityscape of Kyoto, and it is that that influences me most. I think it is dangerous to say what one likes — which building, or which architect, because one doesn't necessarily always know what the purpose or intention of the architect or designer was or is. And if you don't understand that, then you cannot say whether it is good or not. If it were something small, like a phone, say, perhaps I could say something like that, but when I come to something larger, like a building, it becomes more difficult. And while it doesn't specifically have to be the cityscape of Kyoto, I don't think, however, that Tokyo is a beautiful place. But there are other cities in Japan. When you have old cityscapes, like Kyoto, I feel that these can release you. You can just walk through their streets. And the materials or other elements used in the city influence me. Kyoto is older than Tokyo, and a large number of buildings have been preserved in Kyoto, so perhaps that has something to do with it too. the reason. So, I like Kyoto, but it is nothing specific about it. It's something that just exists as part of my daily life that I like about Kyoto.

I enjoy travelling. Being on the way 'there', the trip, the distance to there from here. For example, if I was travelling somewhere, if I was going to Edinburgh, I enjoy the journey *to* Edinburgh and not just Edinburgh itself. I like sitting on the plane and thinking about it. Trying to picture what it will really be like. If I wanted to go to Edinburgh I would look at the cityscape, and I might look at other cities as well, and I would think I might want to go there. But what I really like is the time to think about travelling to a city, because, in the end, I might not go to that city. It is the enjoyment of thinking about going I like.

Ichiro Iwasaki

BrionWega TV products, especially the TV sets designed by Mario Bellini. Also, Bang & Olufsen audio products — they are nearly perfect examples of industrial design.

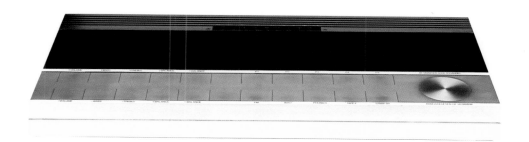

Bang & Olufsen Beomaster 6000, 1976

Sigvard Bernadotte, Bang & Olufsen Beocord Correct Stereo, 1969

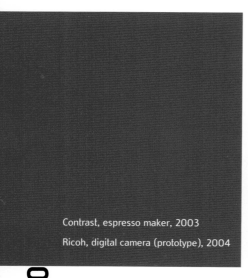

Contrast, espresso maker, 2003

Ricoh, digital camera (prototype), 2004

Ichiro Iwasaki

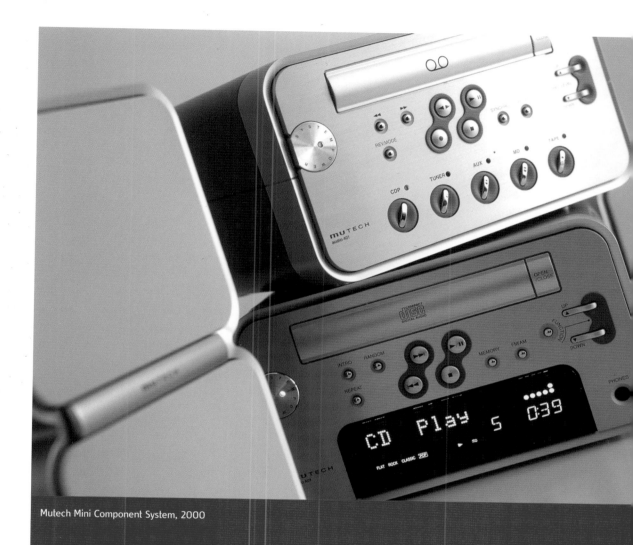

Mutech Mini Component System, 2000

I prefer to read books that are not related to design. For me reading books is a good way to relax and take a break. My favourite authors are Jiro Asada, who writes a lot about how the yakuza interact with kids and people. I love the expressive qualities of Jiro. I also like the late Ryotaro Shiba's work. He has written many good historical novels. Also Nanami Shiono, she is a female author living and working in Italy. And, as I am presently working on tableware, I'm reading a lot of related material, such as *Nihon No Dogu* ("Japanese Tools") or *Cha no Takumi* ("Beauty and Skills of Tea Ceremony").

Ichiro Iwasaki

... Porsche cars always look attractive.
I don't think I want to drive a Porsche. It's an
experience that is very far away from me.

Porsche Carrera GT, 2004

cars

I like car design that exists right now. I also admire the new Mercedes Benz SUV. I think it is beautiful. And Porsche cars always look attractive. I have thought this since I was a child. I don't think I want to drive a Porsche. It's an experience that is very far away from me. When I was child, of course, I could not drive, and I never thought I would be able to drive a Porsche, so it was always something I looked up to. But now I think I would not drive a Porsche. I think it is better enjoyed as a piece of sculpture.

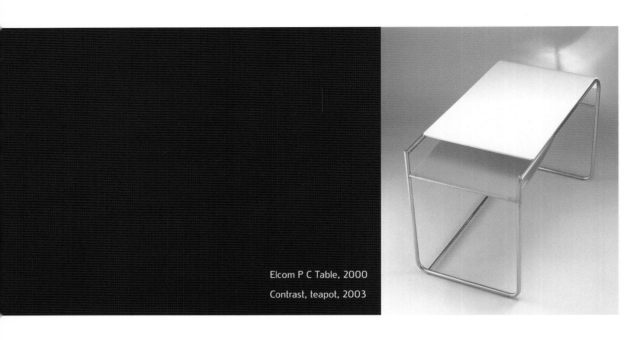

Elcom P C Table, 2000

Contrast, teapot, 2003

Ichiro Iwasaki

Mutech, telephone-answering machine, 2000

I feel that I am never influenced by movies, although there are so many movies that I enjoy. Cinema does not influence my design work, although it may influence me as a person. So, you might say it influences me, in a way. That is the thing, you see, because I do like the film *Blade Runner* and maybe this lay dormant in me. Maybe it is subconscious, or unconscious, I don't know. When I was a student I really admired *Blade Runner*, and I still like it to this day. I read, recently, about Ridley Scott's views on *his* influences. It was interesting to read about this, his Western perspective on Tokyo, and then compare this with the expectations people now have about Tokyo.

> Cinema does not influence my design work, although it may influence me as a person. So, you might say it influences me in a way.

Ichiro Iwasaki

As a designer I am always dealing with the 'reality' of how to make things real. So, it's sometimes hard for me to see art, because I really like the fact that it does not have to be real. It rather challenges me to see art. Art, sometimes, makes me feel that what I am doing is really mundane. In design you have to make things real and I am often limited in that way. I recently watched a TV programme that dealt with the work of Luis Barragan. I now really want to see, with my own eyes, the actual colours he used in Mexico. I love the 'pinkness' — the colour of his work. Barragan is, of course, an architect, but for me he is also an artist. One of the pieces shown in the TV programme was a pond with a pink wall. The colour pink is not a daily colour for me. I have never been to Mexico, but through that TV programme I felt like I had been there. The presenter, who was there, was reporting that the colour pink, which was really pretty shocking, is actually very calming. The whole wall was pink! But apparently, the colour was very calming and soothing. It was really surprising to hear that. This might have been different if it had been in Japan, but because it was Mexico it came across as a calming and soothing colour. And the pink was not just one colour, but layers of different pinks.

I also remember Katsura Funakoshi. He is a Japanese sculptor. I am just fascinated by how his sculptures are full of expressions.

Katsura Funakoshi, Number of Words Arrived, 1991

Ichiro Iwasaki

artists

207

I do not subscribe to any magazines. I don't like magazines as a media, and I look through them only for reference. I buy some magazines on certain occasions, like *AXIS* and *Interni*. *Interni* and *Wallpaper* have more furniture, and so perhaps I enjoy them more. *Interni* is Italian, I think. Otherwise, I just look at magazines and if they interest me I buy them. I sometimes buy Japanese newspapers, but only at the weekend. The newspaper I tend to buy is *Mainichi*.

I have a vast range of musical influences, such as classical, jazz, pop and Japanese regional music called "Okinawa". Right now, however, I think the band Zero 7 are the coolest band around. When I was in Milan recently I went to a music shop and asked someone at the counter what the music was that was playing. It happened to be Zero 7, so I went and brought the CD. But, really, the music I listen to is dependent on what mood I am in and how I feel. This dictates what I listen to. But I don't want to specify a certain genre of music, what I like depends on how I feel. And I feel I am just a normal person.

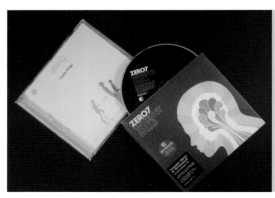

Zero 7, When It Falls,
CD packaging, 2004

Ichiro Iwasaki

Leonardo da Vinci. I think it is impossible for one person to do so many things as he did so well. He is, simply, a genius. His work is great.

In terms of other influential people, I would say the people I talk to, in general, influence me in my design work. Just talking to people influences me the most. Talking helps me design, and I always try to adopt a flexible approach in my work, which is based around the project I'm designing at any one time.

Leonardo da Vinci. I think it is impossible for one person to do so many things as he did so well. He is, simply, a genius. His work is great.

Leonardo da Vinci

Hella Jongerius

Hella Jongerius is a highly influential designer who, in her late 20s, went back to college to study design at the Academy for Industrial Design in Eindhoven, The Netherlands, between 1988 and 1993. There she specialised in textiles, before producing products mainly for the collection of Droog Design. While Jongerius still enjoys a loose association with Droog Design, she set up her own independent design studio, JongeriusLab, in Rotterdam, in 2000.

Jongerius explores the seams between craft, design, and art. When she sets out to create something, she explores what that object means, considering its heritage and archetypes. She often adopts a 'layered' approach in her work, where history and technology, past and present, 'high' and 'low' rub up against one another. Jongerius also manipulates production techniques to create industrialised one-off pieces.

This balance between industrially produced serial objects and handmade unique pieces is a continuing thread throughout Jongerius' work. Re-appropriated combinations between materials and techniques in archetypal shapes are typical of her products. She creates functional objects that are intentionally a bit 'off' — objects where the mistake is cultivated, applauded, and often pursued. Her work is in the collections of the Museum of Modern Art, New York, the Design Museum, London, and the Kunsthal, Rotterdam.

Delft Blue B-Set, 2001

This is a very difficult question for me to answer because I do not have particular designers that I admire. But I do a lot with design from the past, and especially objects from the past. You might call it 'craft', I think. Often, the designer's of these objects didn't have a recognised name, or their names were not as important as names are today. I always look back to the past when I look at form. And I use these forms from the past, but I don't have a big love with the contemporary design field. In terms of the question "Which designers do I really admire?", well, there is some nice stuff being made today, but that's it. I don't have one designer in mind. And there isn't anybody in the design world today whose work I look at and think, "Wow! I wish I had done that." I do not have a role model in that sense. Obviously, when you look around my studio, there are a number of historical artefacts that I collect and use. I find these objects in old museums, in flea markets and antique shops, or wherever. They are 'archetypes' because they are used so much. The forms that we all know and recognise provide us with a kind of memory, and I think what I try to do is work with this kind of archetypal form. For me it's a kind of blank A4 sketch book. So, I have these archetypal forms and I can then add something of our century to them. I can sketch on these forms and use them to give people some recognition of something from the past. Perhaps they had the object at home, or their parents had it, or they saw it in some painting from the mid 1980s.... I then add something that I think is necessary to give it a connection between our time, our world, and the history of the object.

The archetype I work with most is porcelain. Everything, whether it is porcelain or glass, is an archetype. And none of my designs are new forms. So, I do not design any new forms — they are all copies. I start by seeing a technique that I would like to work with, or a material. I work on this aspect first, and then I need a 'form', which is the thing I hate, as it is difficult to make a form for a technique or material. And I don't necessarily believe that we live in a world that needs a new objects — we don't need new forms. But I find a form for what I'm working with. Something needs something long, or something needs something fatter because the material is fat or very poor... and, then, I shop somewhere. I don't have any particular periods or historical references that are favourites. It is always sober. I always take quite an eclectic approach. I go to different museums. I go to museums where there are objects from other countries and cultures, so I get an 'ethnic' outlook, models from other cultures, other worlds. And yeah, that's where I shop. I also do this with fabrics, like the Delft bloom decorations, which are old patterns that have been used for 200 years now. And this kind of painting I use too, and so on. It's a tradition that is alive, from the factory in which it has been used. I use the Dutch blue stuff — all the Delft blue stuff. Like a flower on a very old plate from the seventeenth century. And I blew it up — you change something in only changing its size. You make it more of our time.

Hella Jongerius

Delftware, c. 1660

I have a number of historical artefacts that I collect and use. I find these objects in old museums, in flea markets and antique shops.... They are 'archetypes' because they are used so much. The forms that we all know and recognise provide us with a kind of memory, and I think what I try to do is to work with this kind of archetypal form. For me it's a kind of blank A4 sketchbook.

I take inspiration from the past but I also take inspiration from what is happening right now. And the art world is an inspiration for me, but I also take inspiration from high-tech materials and what you see going on in architecture. And new inventions, the new materials they use for aeroplanes, light materials and materials that can 'breathe'. All of those new inventions are, of course, forms of inspiration. I am thrilled by them, and that is something that inspires me and is often the starting point for an idea.

Before I became a designer, I never went to museums. I am not for old stuff, you know. I am more a girl from the 1980s. I shop around and I know what is going on in the world. I am not just into old stuff. I don't have old stuff in my home but I do use it. I blow dust from it and use it to tell new stories — that is the whole point. But I find inspiration on the streets and in factories — a lot of inspiration in factories, where there are machines that you want to sleep with. And the new Tate, it is one place you simply have to go to — Tate Modern. I love the new Tate. I was there when it opened. It is an open space....

Factory interior, c. 2000

Herzog and de Meuron, Tate Modern, London, 1995–2000

... the art world is an inspiration for me, but I also take inspiration from high-tech materials and what you see going on in architecture. And the new inventions, the new materials they use for aeroplanes....

God, I immediately think of what I use at home. I don't really use my own stuff at home, but then I am always working. I just have some ordinary stuff, just what everybody else has. I am not so into collecting gadgets. As I mentioned earlier, I work a lot with objects from the past. I look back to the past when I am developing a new form. The archetypes I work with most are made of porcelain and glass, everything from water jugs to teapots, cups, and plates. None of my designs are new forms, I don't design new forms — they are all copies, whether they have been found whilst shopping, or whatever.

And, as I also mentioned, I use a lot of fabrics from the past. I won't work with stupid companies with stupid questions. I don't want to be used for my name. I only work on projects that are interesting in the sense that I get *carte blanche*. I don't need a lot of money, but I need money to have my company, the right company, around me. In that sense, maybe I am a little brand. But I want to make interesting work. I think it is very important that I don't stay in one place my whole life. I want to stay small. I don't take on every company that approaches me, or all the money that comes my way. I only take the very interesting stuff. This allows me to be flexible, to design my own world. And it also allows me to choose where I want to work and with whom... to just go out with a laptop and credit card and find new spaces, and new people. That keeps me alive, and awake.

Hella Jongerius

None of my designs are new forms, I do not design new forms — they are all copies, whether they have been found whilst shopping, or whatever.

books

I read a lot of books. But I do not think that it is inspirational to my work as a designer. I read about the world. Oh God, I am always reading about life. I read fiction mostly. I read every evening, as I don't have a television. But I watch TV on the internet — we have a fast internet connection, so I don't have to go through all the shit. I just set what I want to see, so that gives me time to read.

Hella Jongerius

Felt Stool, 2000

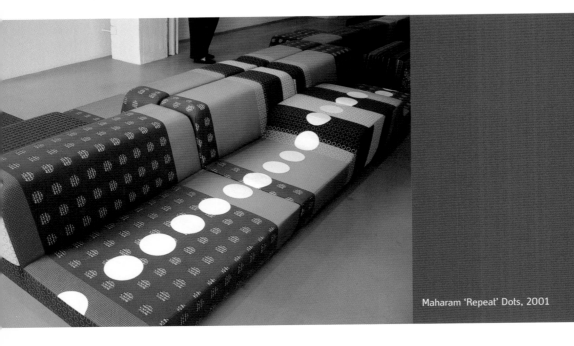

Maharam 'Repeat' Dots, 2001

Hella Jongerius

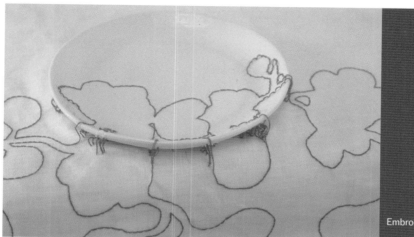

Embroidered Tablecloth, 2000

Long Neck and Groove Bottle, 2000

Elements from the exhibition 'Repeat', 2002

cars

Car? I bet Marcel Wanders mentioned a Porsche. I like cars. I am looking for a new car, and I am always looking at Mercedes cars. Mercedes is a kind of archetype — this kind of big, over-the-top big truck I really like. But I can't afford one myself. We were looking for a car and I said to my love that I want a Mercedes. I would like a new one — the biggest one available. But, you know, I don't believe in old time. We don't drive in a museum, so I would take the newest one, *and* I would also take the archetypal Mercedes.

cinema

Yeah, somedays I get inspiration from the cinema. I am not so good in that field — not so good with names. What was the last movie I saw? I think it was called *Venture of Heaven*. I liked it. I also read the book. And, of course, I saw *Harry Potter* recently. What do I like at the movies? I cannot say that I have one genre, one director, somebody that I really admire. I see all kinds of films, but I don't have particular heroes.

Hella Jongerius

Wim Delvoye. He is a Belgian artist. What he does, and what I really like about what he does, is he takes tradition out of his work. For example, he made this very big truck in concrete with this very big round thing on the back, and then he totally covered the roof with a material that was out of context. What he does is use tradition and traditional crafts, but uses them in unusual contexts. He has a totally different way of looking at the materials and scale of craft, and then he connects these different worlds. That is what I really like about his work. And I like Atelier van Lieshout. I like his work because he has this dirty kind of approach, this roughness. There is something very 'archetypical' of his big scale way of doing things, which crosses the border of art and design. This is also what I like about his work. Atelier Van Lieshout, like Wim Delvoye, works on this edge.

I like being on this edge, too. I always call myself a designer, and I am, because I am in love with the process — the industrial process. It is the feeling I get, which I really like, from the industrial process after making a prototype. I always start with making a prototype. And, then, you have a unique cup, or whatever, and only then do I decide whether this is a product to make in series. I then decide how big to make the series — five or ten or 20 or 100,000, or more if it is for a big company. I like it when a product is more than one. Otherwise it is an object. And I like the follow-up, because then you make a product more 'adult' and you have to work within industrial rules. Industrial rules are completely different than those for unique objects, and I like that. But I don't like the compromises of the industrial process. I like it to go as far as you can and traverse the borders of whatever the field. This is what I want to say about industrialisation — that it is so perfect now, and everything you want you can buy. The industrial revolution is finished, so we don't have to develop anything anymore — it's all perfect. We can make anything, produce everything perfectly, with a good price. But I think consumers want something else. I think they want unique pieces that are industrially made — otherwise you buy art. So, is it possible to make and produce designed objects using an industrial process and for them to be unique pieces? In some of my work, that is the goal I want to achieve. That is another connection. So there are connections, and some of my products are about the past, some are about the past and the future, and some are about whether they are industrial or unique pieces. The tension between these borders is something that I like playing with.

The industrial revolution is finished, so we don't have to develop anything anymore — it's all perfect. We can make anything, produce everything perfectly with a good price. But I think consumers want something else.

Wim Delvoye,
Caterpillar Scale
Model No 4, 2002

Hella Jongerius

Pushed Washtub, 1995

Hella Jongerius

Blizzard Bulbs, 2002

Kasese Sheep Chair, 1999

Hella Jongerius

I read the newspaper every day from the first sentence to the last. If I settle on the Internet, I always watch specific things, and I know exactly what is going on in the world. I want to know, as I am part of the world. And I use this information as the whole theme of being an individual is sometimes reflected in my work. My work is always about, maybe not functionality, but feeling or being with someone socially — or not. But I like to give materials some humanity, to make them not so cold. Although I don't know how to connect this with the everyday. I like BBC News and CNN, and the Dutch newspaper *NRC*. But I don't like when movies are only about the past, or have a story about the past. I like layers in movies, and layers in news. And if I look at art, things on TV, shows or exhibitions, documentaries or whatever, there are always these layers. Being in time and doing something in time, what is going on now, that is something I am really interested in.

I have got a lot of press recently, but I never do anything for the press. They always come. And I don't complain. I think I need to be in the press, as my work is not in every shop as sometimes I only produce three or four pieces in a series. And sometimes I only show work in exhibition, so I need the press. But sometimes it's too much. And I think it is not so hip anymore to be in every magazine, to do that kind of shit. I think it is overrated and over-the-top. But we are now in this world where shopping is *the* big hobby for everybody, and someone has to make the meat for it. Somebody has to make stuff so that everybody can shop. And so we, as designers, make it. And, with shopping, we are the ones that are in those magazines. It is not that we are so very interesting, it is just what is now and here. And I need it, but I am not a big fan of all this.

I have just been to Brazil, so I bought a lot of Brazilian music. I can dance to that music. I like Brazilian dance music. But, you know, I have also got loads of African music, as I was in Africa a lot. And, of course, when I go out dancing, I like to dance to all the new DJ stuff, like St Germain. But again, I don't know all the names.

If you saw my music collection, it is like... oh, there is everything. If I go to a different country I always buy the labels from that country. And I look at what is going on nowadays, and buy that too. But classical music I do not do, and country music also I do not like.

St Germain, Tourist,
CD cover, 2000

Well, I think I would take a political person from the past to give me some happiness, and have a nice time with, but who? This is a hard question. I need some time to think about it....

Hella Jongerius

RADI

The members of the group RADI Designers work together on a variety of projects covering product, exhibition and interior design. As a group and individually, they both reply to specific client briefs and propose new objects or ideas.

RADI Designers play with the evidences of daily life, gestures and object-product-furniture-gadget typologies, manipulating and reworking codes, uses, techniques and forms, in an attempt to constantly reinvent the existing. The different qualities of RADI objects are not immediately perceptible, they require a gradual discovery, made by touching, feeling or quite simply walking around the object. There is no obvious formal family likeness, the link lies in the characteristics that they share; the hidden dimension of their use, the stimulation of the senses and an underlying humour.

RADI have worked for a diverse range of clients, including Marlboro, Air France, Schweppes, and Issey Miyake. Their creative output has featured in a number of books, catalogues, and magazine articles. RADI's work is also in the permanent collection of several prominent museums throughout the world including the Centre Georges Pompidou, Paris, the Cartier Foundation, Paris, and the Musee du Design, Lisbon, Portugal.

Fabulation Installation, Foundation Cartier pour l'A

Olivier Sidet: In the beginning, we worked on real products, but we exhibited them in art galleries and we approached them in a way that you wouldn't expect. However, we were also very precise. So, you would have, like, real nice technical drawings going on with the most absurd ideas. We mixed the two. It was not a sculpture, it was not a comment, and not a product.

Florence Doleac: The message we wanted to give was that it was not necessary to be too serious. To be professional you have to be serious in the office, but the product, I think, can be more fun.

Olivier: I think it was more the other way round. I think we are very serious when we work, but the message in the product does not have to reflect the seriousness, the hard work and the serious approach that we give to the product. And actually, sometimes when people come to work in our office they are quite surprised by the silence that there can be for a whole day, because everyone is concentrating and working. Students, when they come to see us, they only knew our objects, and they think there is a constant party here.

Florence: We are not so funny as individuals, so it's a bit disappointing to some people. You come here and you discover that behind this product, there are quite boring people.

Olivier: We said we wanted to do all kinds of products and wanted to approach them all in the same way. Which means we do not want to privilege mass production, and we don't want to privilege handmade gallery works. And this is really something that has worked. But from the beginning on, we have worked with galleries and museums *and* industrial producers, all at the same time.

Anyway, I can start with Allesandro Mendini. I saw an exhibition of his work only yesterday. What is interesting about Mendini is that he works on two levels — theoretical and practical. And, I think, the things he makes are not below what he is saying, which is what can happen sometimes when people who write start to make things. So, for me, if I look at the person and I see these two levels, what he says and what he does, it's interesting. Whenever I see the work of designers that just design things, I can really appreciate the objects, but if there is not a story, some theory, some thought, then, for me, there is always something missing.

There are several Mendini projects I really admire, and I look at him more than I look at artists. There is not one single project that I really love. But his work, and once again, the way he approaches his work, is what I like. If you look at a book of Mendini's work, it's more than a single project that is interesting about it. He takes different approaches where he produces a series of objects that are, how do you say, demure testimonies of his thoughts. And these thoughts can be about a family of objects, or they can be about what is serious and what is a game. I would have liked to have found a kind of 'God' of design, a kind of model, when I was a student. You always look around and say what you want to do, what kind of design and how you want to do it. But I never found it.

If I look at products, products that have influenced me in a very indirect way, I would say the work of Dennis Santachiara has influenced me. As a designer he's quite well known, but he was much more in the media in the 1980s. What fascinates me most about some of Santachiara's products is that they were totally out of style, like you don't know who designed these things. They were totally unfashionable somehow. And these shapes, I looked at them and I liked them. They were pretty unique. You could not say this is part of, whatever, organic or minimalist design, it was just very bizarre and I was always intrigued by that, because he was playing in the same field as everyone else, being published in the same magazines, and being present Milan, and so on. But there were these strange objects, and I never understood how someone could really like these products as they were *too* strange. If you look at best-selling products, they are never really strange, they are usually 'soft' design. So, Santachiara's products made me think of when I was in school. And then there are things that I like simply because they are beautiful. It is like having a coffee and a girl passes by — you are happy to see that.

Alessandro Mendini,
Proust's Armchair, 1978

Florence: I am always curious about what Frank Gehry is doing... and Renzo Piano. That's all. I am interested in their work. I think the diversity of Renzo Piano's work is amazing. I would like to see New Caledonia, one of his late projects — it seems very strange. As for Frank Gehry, I would like to see his Guggenheim Museum in Bilbao, because it too seems to be quite strange.

I am curious about whether the Guggenheim really works or not, as I hear from other architects that cubic rooms were used for exhibition spaces. This sounds very bizarre to me. Antonio Gaudi uses the same language inside and out. And then he makes a picture of the outside. I would be disappointed if this were what was done at the Guggenheim. But I don't really know where architecture is going today. I heard Jean Nouvel recently saying that you can be employed nowadays just to design the picture of a building — the outside, or the 'skin' — and the rest is done by anybody. And architects accept this, because they can. But it's very strange to me to think that you can just do the skin of a building. I don't like that.

Olivier: I have a big problem with architecture. When we mention design and it being hard to just admire an object... for me architecture is even more difficult to admire in this way. I have a total disregard for architecture, for contemporary architecture. I rarely like any of it. Although I do like some of the odd architectural projects by Frank Gehry. I like these more as objects. I am not sure that I like them as architecture. But Gehry is really exceptional.

The problem with architecture for me is that it's always very, very deadly serious. Maybe this is because there is so much money involved. When I feel good in architectural spaces it is usually because there is some sort of bricolage going on, when there are things happening that were not foreseen, that have happened by chance. Or when you are in a country that is not so industrialised and the people invent things with the buildings there being somehow very free and open. You can find this in Italy, in Thailand, wherever.... But the well-known, big architects with lots of money who build villas for, I don't know, for me? These projects are always failures. They are too perfect.

I have a big problem with architecture. When we mention design and it being hard to just admire an object... for me architecture is even more difficult to admire in this way. I have a total disregard for architecture, for contemporary architecture. I rarely like any of it.

Olivier: I cannot admire a product. I can only admire a person. A product is always just a product and if it is not part of a story, then it can be nice, beautiful, intelligent, and even successful, but it remains a thing, a little thing.

Florence: I agree. It's difficult. I don't have a product in mind. If I see something, for sure, yeah, but I am more influenced by people. Looking at people, how they work, how they walk, and all their gestures. I am more fascinated by life — the life of birds, cats and people.

Olivier: I mean, how can you admire a product? A product can be very well designed, and maybe we are happy it is here — or maybe we are not happy because we have to use it all day. Anyway, it has an impact. But, there's no question, you cannot admire this 'thing'. When you start studying, maybe, and you say, I want to design something like this... but when you start thinking a bit more, you can really only admire people. In saying this again, though, I think Gehry's furniture is great.

Florence: He is the only architect that is able to make nice furniture.

Olivier: I would like people to pay homage to some of our products — the Whippet Bench, for example, we were always playing with the status symbol of this object. The Whippet Bench has this funny thing about it, there is a surrealistic thing to it and, at the same time, it is intended for a collectors market. It's serious and it's expensive, and very well made. We are happy about this product, as it has entered the 'real' world. This is about admiration, it beig sold at auction, whatever. On the other hand, it is a dog, and you sit on the dog's back. So it's not something that is hyper-cool, it's not a hyper-cool shape, there's something surrealist and strange about it. And I think this association makes it richer. That's what I like about it. So, it's not *so* serious.

> ... I am more influenced by people. Looking at people, how they work, how they walk, and all their gestures. I can only be fascinated by life — the life of birds, cats and people.

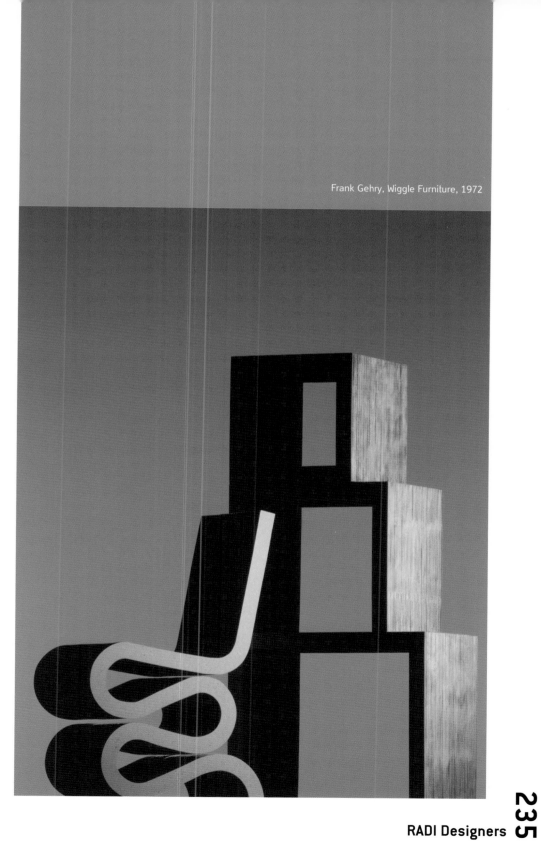

Frank Gehry, Wiggle Furniture, 1972

RADI Designers

Olivier: I don't have much time to read. I don't read very much.

Florence: I do. It is important to me. I have periods when I spend a lot of time reading, and I read particular things. Then I have periods where everything is disorganised and I read nothing, and I don't go out. It's not structured. But I really like biographies. I read, for example, Dali's biography, *The Secret Life of Salvador Dali*, in which he wrote a lot about his life when he was a young man. It's interesting, the relationships he kept throughout his life, through his work and the people he came into contact with. Now, I am reading a book by Umberto Eco.

Olivier: We don't only share the same TV, but also the last book. *The Secret Life of Salvador Dali* was the last book I really liked, yeah. And I've recently read some scientific books about how our brains work. But I don't read much, and my reading isn't very consistent. And I don't read fiction, almost never.

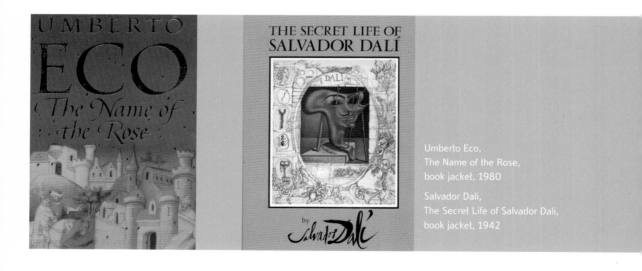

Umberto Eco,
The Name of the Rose,
book jacket, 1980

Salvador Dali,
The Secret Life of Salvador Dali,
book jacket, 1942

Florence: For me, the car I like most is the QuatreL. It is the Renault 4L.

Olivier: 4L. It's very famous. The QuatreL.

Florence: It's nearly disappeared in the last ten years. Now you never see them. But they were really cool. Everybody had one. It was very common. It really influenced me because my grandfather gave me one when I got my driving licence. I had real fun driving it. It was very 'soft', it was like a filter. Then, I think any kind of car is a filter; they make you stupid... the attitude of people to their cars, it is amazing! But a QuatreL was a good influence because it put you in a good mood. You can't be too serious in a QuatreL. You can't get nervous. I also liked the Citröen 2CV. Again, you can't be too serious with this car either. And I like this relationship when moving in space. In these cars you keep your elasticity, you are ridiculous. So the QuatreL, this ridiculous car, is very important to me.

Olivier: For me, it's very simple, actually. I had a Volkswagen Beetle. And as I was not born in France, but in Austria, there is parallel between the Beetle and the QuatreL. My mother's first car was a Beetle, and we used it to go on holidays together. I think the Beetle provides a very similar experience to the QuatreL. You know, going to Italy with my mother in the Beetle full of holiday stuff and there are all of these cars passing us by....

Citröen 2CV, c. 1980

Volkswagen Beetle, c. 1980

RADI Designers

Olivier: I would say for me that it has to be Stanley Kubrick — all of his work! I am an unconditional fan of Kubrick. *Eyes Wide Shut* is his best film, the last one is always the best. It's a very 'strong' film. If you look at Kubrick's production, from one movie to another, it's incredible how free he was in his approach to such different themes and atmospheres. His genius wasn't just his intellectual side, but his writing too, which is amazing. It's like there is nothing more to say. And every time you watch one of his films the effect is totally fantastic and unexpected.

Florence: Well, I really like Kubrick too. Because we have the same TV and watch the same films we get the same influences from movies. And I'm really always very excited to see the films of Pedro Almodovar. In terms of actors, my favourite is Christopher Walken. He is really cool.

the ultimate trip

Stanley Kubrick, 2001: A Space Odyssey, promotional postcard, 1968

2001: A SPACE ODYSSEY
MGM PRESENTS THE STANLEY KUBRICK PRODUCTION

Whippet Bench, 1998

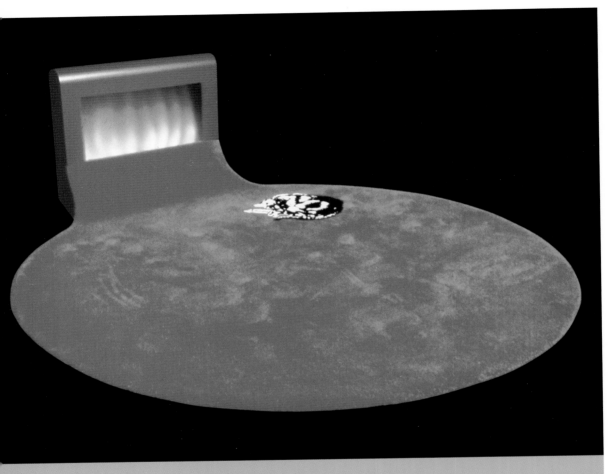

Sleeping Cat Rug, 1999

Ghost Miroir, 2001

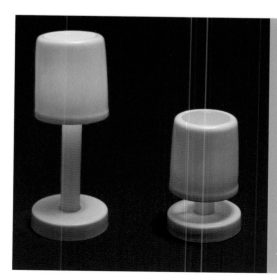

Abat Jour Pour Bougie Candleholder Lamp, 1999

Olivier: For me, art is like design, which means it has the same place in my head as design. It's not above it and it's not underneath it. And it's not part of this group of direct emotional influences, like music or cinema. For me, art is like design. I saw the work of Bruce Nauman recently at a big exhibition in the Centre Pompidou, and even though I didn't know his work that well it was extremely strong. It was kind of a surprise, as I had never seen this work before.

Florence: Yes, I like Nauman too. But I also love the work of Alain Sechas, a French artist. He is a contemporary artist who paints and makes videos and sculptures. And Pierrick Sorin, a young French artist. His work is very French. He makes a lot of jokes, but somehow his installations are quite complex, with a lot of effects — videos and all kinds of transformations, transforming pictures. And he acts in his work too, always playing different roles.

Olivier: He is a great actor actually.

Florence: ... always perfect. He can play any role: serious, 'political', stupid. He did this thing that really made us laugh recently, but I think a lot of people don't really accept this kind of thing as art. You know, if it's funny it is not artistic. But his work is special because it's really on the edge.

Olivier: When you look at these videos you really laugh like when watching a good comic. And he puts you in a position where you're asking, "Is this really art when I'm laughing with my hands on my knees?" He is really good. Then there is Orozco, Gabriel Orozco. He does a lot of photo work. He did a very famous piece where he cut a Citröen DS in two and then stuck it back together with the middle section removed. And he does a lot of photographic work, almost documentary work, but influenced by his special viewpoint. I think he is Mexican or Latin. Yeah, subtraction — his work is about removing things. The Citröen DS is actually a very special object, and when you look at his work in general you understand why he did it. But if you only know this one piece, you might just think it's okay. You know, a quick idea... just a fast idea to do this. But when you see this piece along with the rest of his work, it becomes quite calm — a very nice work.

Florence: But emotion and art, I get more from portrait painting, particularly from the Baroque period. This type of painting I could live with. Their colours would bring something to each day that would change my mood and inspire me. It's like the painting travelling in time and space. I don't have this feeling when I see an exhibition nowadays. Usually, they are very aggressive with their message. It's too much.

Olivier: A particular favourite from the Italian Renaissance is Piero della Francesca. We also adore Géricault. And we also get a similar feeling, even if it is much less realistic, from Greek religious art and antique mosaics.

... art is like design, which means it has the same place in my head as design. It's not above it and it's not underneath it. And it's not part of this group of direct emotional influences, like music or cinema. For me, art is like design.

Jean-Louis-André-Théodore Géricault,
A Horse frightened by Lightning, c. 1813–1814

Olivier: I look at magazines, but I don't really read them.

Florence: Sometimes I read scientific magazines, but not regularly....

Olivier: I would say we read newspapers more than magazines. Magazines we just flick through. But we don't read specific magazines or newspapers religiously.

Olivier: This is actually very easy for me. I really love the music of Beck. There is a programme called Music Planet TV that screens once a week on RTE. And each week there is a documentary about a musician shown. I love these programmes. All the background stories bring an extra dimension to the music. For example, I didn't know about Beck's background in fine art, and that his grandfather was one of the founders of Fluxus. It's only then that you understand things differently. And last week there was a programme about Roxy Music, which was great.

Florence: Roxy Music are really great. And all the stories of the group's break-ups and comebacks. They are really smart. Bryan Ferry is really smart.

Olivier: And there was also a programme on Abba. You got to see the whole story of Abba. It's an amazing story.

Florence: You know, you know the music and you like it, and then suddenly you can see the people behind the scenes.

Olivier: So, we are kind of passive consumers. I also love Ween. Have you heard of them? They are twins, or brothers or something — Gene and Dean Ween.

Roxy Music, Country Life, CD cover, 1974
ABBA, The Best of ABBA, CD cover, 2000

Olivier: I think Ronald Biggs, the great train robber, is a great figure. Even though he is a thief, he is someone we both admire a lot. And after reading Salvador Dali's biography, he's a person that we would very much have liked to meet.

Florence: We'd really like to share dinner with Ronnie Biggs and Roman Polanski. This would be a very interesting evening.

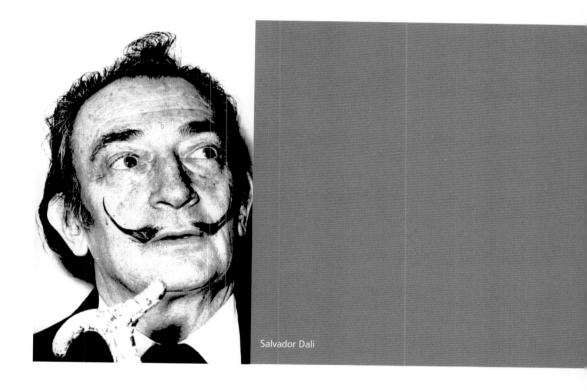

Salvador Dali

Karim Rashid

Karim Rashid was born in Cairo, Egypt in 1960; half English, half Egyptian and raised mostly in Canada. In 1982 he received a Bachelor of Industrial Design from Carleton University, Ottawa, Canada. He then moved to Milan for a year at the Rodolfo Bonetto Studio. On his return to Canada, he worked for seven years with KAN Industrial Designers.

Rashid opened his own practice in New York City in 1993, and has since worked for numerous clients globally, such as Umbra, Prada, Yahoo!, Magis, Issey Miyake, Totem, Guzzini, Estee Lauder, Tommy Hilfiger, Giorgio Armani, Sony, Zanotta, and YSL, amongst others.

Rashid has over 70 objects in permanent collections worldwide, and his work has been exhibited at the Philadelphia Museum of Art, Museum of Modern Art, New York, San Francisco Museum of Modern Art, Museum of Decorative Arts, Montreal, Cooper-Hewitt National Design Museum, New York, and the Design Museum, London.

Blobject Chair, 1999

My father has a very interesting background. He was a painter and a set designer for film and television. He also spent a large part of his life studying, doing his doctorate, so I grew up with a lot of pencils, paint and paper lying around as a child. One of the first things I learned was documentation, the reaction to life around you, trying to interpret and personalise things. I used to get ideas down on paper. So, I had a very artistic upbringing. Artists like Picasso and Brancusi, all these kinds of people inspired me greatly. And around the age of 12, 13 or 14, I started to enjoy the work of designers more, and started reading about them. I have been inspired and influenced by many designers, including Bruno Munari, Gio Ponti, Joe Columbo, and Gaetano Pesce. Then, at school I became interested in the work of Italian designers, like the Italian radical design movement of the 1970s: UFO, Superstudio and Ettore Sottsass. I also admired Archigram, from the UK, at this time. By the time I finished my undergraduate studies, I was determined I was going to go and work in Italy and learn from the Italians. I ended up going there and studying under Pesce and Sottsass. I had read a lot about them and researched their ideas, and what occurred to me most is that it wasn't their work so much, but their approach or philosophy of design that was most important. For example, I have just read a number of biographies, including Andy Warhol's, which is fantastic, and through these you understand how these great artists and designers saw life. That is why I think every designer is capable of good and bad, and if you look at their work, rather than judge it, one minute they have done something fantastic and the next minute it is not necessarily that good. This, I feel, is a better way of understanding what their vision and comprehension of culture and society was or is.

In terms of contemporaries, there are some designers who are doing fantastic things. For instance, I admire the work of Ross Lovegrove. He is a good friend. I feel we share a certain symbiosis in our work. I admire him for the organic sensibility in his designs. I think there is new territory to do new things in design nowadays. I have always been an advocate of design theory and, as such, have studied the work of Heidegger amongst others. In my teaching activities I tell my students to understand the world first. I think design is a political act. It is a social act. Any experience is a good experience. There are two important things you can learn in design — dialogue and theory.

Karim Rashid

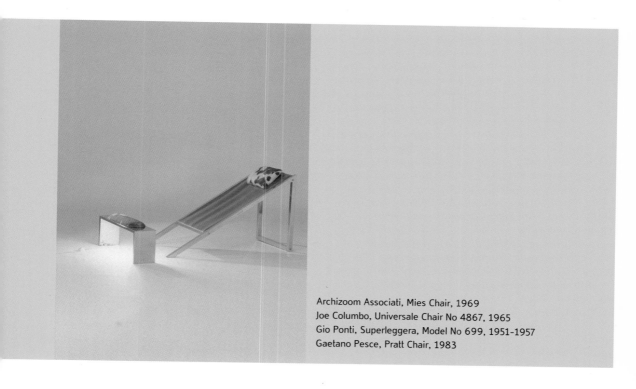

Archizoom Associati, Mies Chair, 1969
Joe Columbo, Universale Chair No 4867, 1965
Gio Ponti, Superleggera, Model No 699, 1951-1957
Gaetano Pesce, Pratt Chair, 1983

buildings

There are certain architects that I think are truly fantastic, such as Neutra. I also admire the organic movement in architecture. I have a bias towards organic architecture. Saarinen's TWA terminal in New York is fantastic. I think that the shifting space through the organic form is beautiful. I have this fascination and obsession with the Kit House by Buckminster Fuller, and Fuller's work in general, his idea of a house as a kit of parts, a house as a package that you buy. I love the idea of the building as kit. The next step for me is to do installations, and what I want to develop, what I want to do is a kit building — a plastic house. What I want to do is buy some land and build myself a plastic house. My brother, Hani Rashid, has a practice called Asymptote, in Philadelphia, that is doing some interesting things. My favourite house project is Pierre Cardin's Riviera house, the Palais de Bulles.

Buckminster Fuller,
Geodesic Dome, c. 1970

Karim Rashid

This profession is so fucked up — it's so full of jealousies and so full of personalities and recriminations. The reality is in Europe, where design is always part of everyday life, more or less. Design has become a social discussion — it's really on peoples' minds nowadays. I really loved a range of products by a group called Water Studio. I think they are a Japanese company that did limited editions of a car called Escargot and a camera for Olympus called the Ecru. The camera is also a limited edition. I adored the little red cosmetic ball for Miyake — the Fire cosmetic bottle. There's a clear camera for Konica that is beautiful, as is the i–Zone camera. I love the telephone that Starck did for Philips/Alessi that looks like a snail. I think it's great. Bang & Olufsen have done some beautiful stuff. Their 1974 stereo, BO 2400, with the first remote, is one of my favourite pieces of industrial design. But the more I travel the world, the more I realise this profession is full of competitiveness and jealousy. The problem with the past is that the tendency is to work off the archetype. If you look at the magnificent Michael Thonet Number 14 Chair, for example, and bent wood chairs in general — forget the archetype! You may be using bent wood, but look at how people sit! In industrial design, we have a tendency to believe that it is an artistic profession, so we deny the commoditisation of the business. We often live in denial. I also admire the Avanti car by Raymond Loewy, Paco Rabanne's cosmetic bottle, circa 1973, and Dieter Rams' Stereo, circa 1967.

Michael Thonet, No 14 Chair, 1858

Bang & Olufsen Beomaster 1900, 1976

Time and Space, 2003

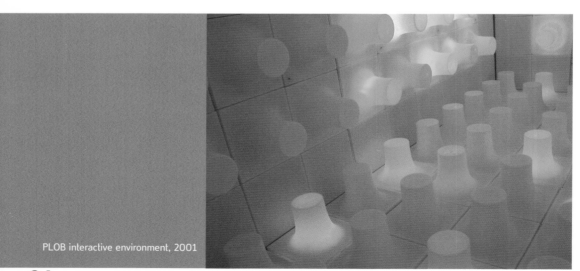

PLOB interactive environment, 2001

Karim Rashid

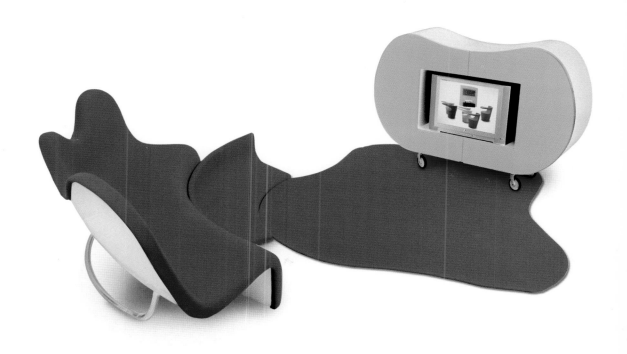

Chrysalis and Butterfly, 2003

I'm not a big fiction reader. I still read a lot of design theory and in the last two years I have been reading a lot of business books. I really enjoyed the book *Glamorama*. The author of *American Psycho* wrote it. He also wrote *Less than Zero*. I have just finished reading Miles Davis' autobiography. It was amazing! Right now I am reading a lot of business and marketing textbooks. As with art, it's the same with music and literature. I am trying to focus only on things that are new for me. I really don't want to go back. I feel I have done that. I have read all the books and seen all the stuff. So I read and listen to stuff that is less than five years old. It's all about working in the moment! I would also add to this list Hal Foster's books *The Anti-Aesthetic* and *Design and Crime*, Nietzsche's *Beyond Good and Evil*, and Guy Debord's *Society of the Spectacle*.

Bret Easton Ellis,
American Psycho,
book jacket, 1991

Dann & Dann,
Introduction to Marketing,
book jacket, 2004

At the moment I really love small European cars. The Smart by Mercedes, I love it. I was in Italy a couple of days ago and I saw one — it was so cute. I like these kinds of nifty little cars. Some of them are no bigger than this table but they can hold up to four people — amazing! My sensibility in car design at the moment is hyper-efficiency. I also saw a car recently when I was abroad — it looked like a little box. I think it might have been called the A2. I think Audi make it. Yeah, the Audi A2 — that looks like a great little car.

But I don't really like cars in general (I am a big advocate of public transportation) — although a few have always intrigued me, such as Loewy's Avanti, the Rolls Royce Camargue, designed by Pinafarina, the Honda Cube, the Scion xb and the Jaguar E-type.

Smart, 2003

I love David Lynch movies — his portrayal of
a lonely, sick America. I used to be big fan of
old European movies, but most European
movies nowadays are really boring — they
are just terrible.

cinema

I love David Lynch movies — his portrayal of a lonely, sick America. I used to be big fan of old European movies, but most European movies nowadays are really boring — they are just terrible. Hollywood movies are now so seductive. In saying that, however, one of my all-time favourite European movies is *Until the End of the World* by Wim Wenders. And I adored the movie *Hard Eight*. I also love the early Coen brothers' movies. I adore the movie *The Cell* with Jennifer Lopez, which has truly amazing visuals — great costumes, make-up and colour. I loved all the costumes in that movie. *Tron* is also a great favourite of mine — it has that 'in your face' level of technology. I also think the movies *American Beauty*, *The Virgin Suicides*, and *Poison* were great, but I wouldn't class them as hugely influential. I stayed up all night three months ago watching these movies back to back. They are hugely enjoyable films and great examples of what Hollywood can do these days. The movies that I remember years later are films that have really motivated, inspired, and engaged me. Many of the films I watch I forget completely. And few films touch a deep emotive response in me, but some that have include *Herostratus*, *Solaris* (the original version), *Monster*, *Eyes of Laura Mars*, and *American Gigolo*.

Karim Rashid

I'm from an artistic background. I grew up in a very creative environment around artistic materials. I grew up at a young age to love artists like Andre Lott, Géricault and Isamu Noguchi. Personally, I have a bias towards amorphic form, and when I look back now I realise that artists like Noguchi, Jean Arp and the whole organic movement I discovered as a teenager and an undergraduate were inspirational. I really admire the organic qualities in Arp's work. I also love the work of Peter Halley — a contemporary American artist. His work is fantastic. I guess it's a kind of tech-teeny thing. I'm really into these American post-graffiti artists, such as TEK — I think they have the same sensibility that I do, they use these fluorescent colours and the same energy that I use in my work. I call this the "infostatic". I'm trying now to focus only on contemporary work, to only see things that are 'new'. I made a decision a few years ago not to have anything in my house that is more than five years old, no literature or music that is more than five years old. I really need to do this post-American refugee thing. I want to see if I can live totally in the contemporary world. There is this saying: "Artists don't see the future. They only see the present." I don't know who said it, but it's one of the best things that I've ever heard.

Personally, I have a bias towards amorphic form, and when I look back now I realise that artists like Isamu Noguchi, Jean Arp and the whole organic movement I discovered as a teenager and undergraduate were inspirational.

Bloob Pedestal, 2004

Fessura Mirror, 2004

Picnic Bag, 2003

One of my favourite magazines is *Numero* — it's kind of lifestyle, culture, fashion rolled into one. *Wallpaper* is really aggressive — I find it amateur. *Numero* is not at all; it's more contemporary. It is pure nostalgia. *Fad* is a great magazine. As is *Pop*. I love fashion magazines. I get *Vogue*, *Marie Claire*, and *Elle*. I also read *The New York Times* and *USA Today* regularly.

I like a lot of French disco, guys like Bob Sinclair. I also listen a lot to Baby Memeth. I really like Dirk Diggler. I also really like St Germain at the moment. Currently, jazz and trip-hop are my favourites. Maybe this has something to do with me once being a buyer in a jazz shop. Years back I was a really big jazz fan, probably about 17 to 18 years ago. I have a long list of musical heroes — The Crusaders, Herbie Hancock, George Duke, Miles Davis, Lonnie Liston Smith, Donald Byrd, Burt Bacharach, Dionne Warwick, Olivia Newton John, John Denver, Bruce Cockburn, Chicago, James Taylor, and West Coast music, such as Orleans, Bobby Caldwell, Kenny Loggins, Michael Franks, Gerry Rafferty, and Christopher Cross. Also some of the founders of electronic dance music, such as Giorgio Moroder, Kraftwerk, Alan Parsons, Human League and Roxy Music.

I love music. I always equate designing with a great democratic object like writing a hit pop song. Few people can do it and when it happens it is an amazing feeling that you can have such an impact on our collective public memory.

Karim Rashid

In terms of historical figures that I admire, I would have to say David Bowie and Andy Warhol. There are so many people that I find influential, but I would limit it to these two as the most influential for me.

There are many, many people that I would love to have to dinner. If I had to make a choice, though, I'd really like to have dinner with Damien Hirst. I'd like to ask him where he gets his great ideas from. Pablo Picasso would also be a great dinner companion. I think John Paul Gaultier would also have to be there. Philippe Starck would be great. I met my talking match the day I met Philippe Starck. Lastly, I would have Kevin Spacey. Every film he has been in I have loved, I think he is such a great actor, and I would really love to meet and talk to him.

I would also say individuals like Rodchenko, Yves Saint Laurent, and Pierre Cardin. And great philosophers and writers, such as Paul Virilio, Jean Baudrillard, Jacques Derrida, Lyotard, Hal Foster, Martin Heidegger, and Foucault.

I met my talking match the day I met Philippe Starck.

Andy Warhol
Kevin Spacey
Damian Hirst

Tejo Remy

Tejo Remy studied at the College for the Fine Arts in Utrecht, The Netherlands. Remy graduated from the 3-D Design Department in 1991. Remy's final project work at Utrecht consisted of his now famous chest of drawers, milk bottle lamp, and rag chair. These pieces, which were quickly snapped up by Droog Design for their collection, centred around the theme of Robinson Crusoe's island, with Remy improvising his designs using materials and objects that lay at hand.

Part of Remy's work comprises a revolt against trendy design, but it is also because he feels existing, or 'found' objects add an extra dimension to contemporary design. But Tejo Remy's works are not only assembled out of re-appropriated objects and materials, they also represent a collection of memories.

Droog Design earned him much publicity and an international reputation, and as a result he has received numerous commissions, ranging from building installations to product design.

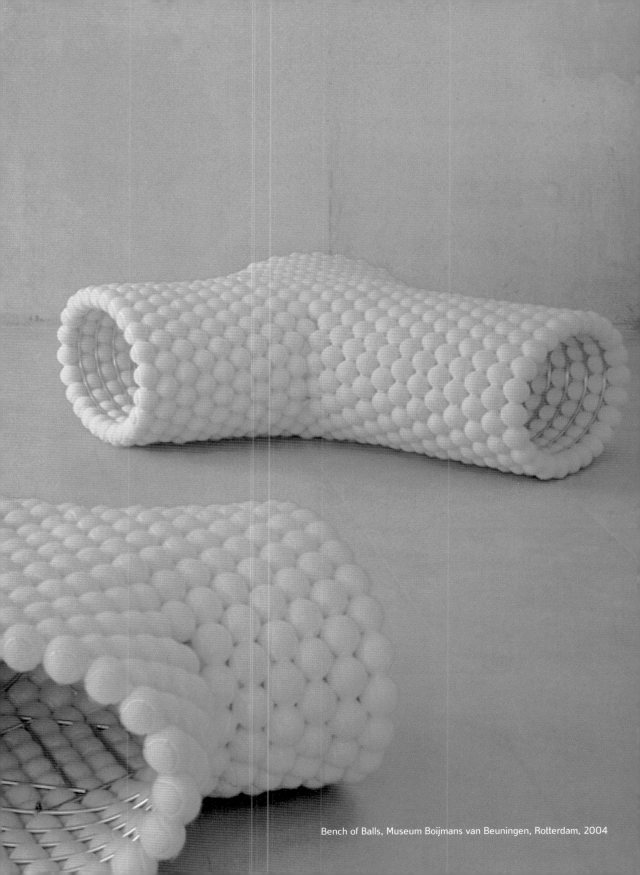

Bench of Balls, Museum Boijmans van Beuningen, Rotterdam, 2004

It is easy to start in the past, you know. I start there because it was in the late 1980s when there was this, how do you call them, this group in Germany. You know the work of Stiletto? They made a chair out of a shopping trolley, so there is a resemblance there with my early work in a way. I admire this approach of making things that you find through a kind of anti-consumerist behaviour. This is what I am trying to do.

I graduated in 1991, and I started designing right away. In those days there was this issue about the environment — ecological design. The things that I picked up then, for me it was not about the environment, but it was more like Robinson Crusoe. Crusoe got stranded on an island, and he had to make his own paradise. He had to make this with what he found, and in that way I did the same with my early pieces, such as the Rag Chair and the Milk Bottle Lamp. With the chest of drawers, You Can't Lay Down Your Memories, there is another story. It took two years into that project before I found the way to visualise the workings of the open memory. Each drawer has its own identity, because they have to work from a social dimension, a way of activating your memory. How the memory feels is put in the object, and the object, in turn, is put in the house. And those objects are memory related. It is the same as with a conventional chest of drawers, in that each drawer has its own identity.

About the same time as being influenced by Stiletto I admired the work of the Pentagram Design Company. I don't know the names of the designers in Pentagram, but I admired their way of putting things together — two hours together on a project and that's it, end solution. Yeah, this smooth, slick approach, the way many Italian designers work.

So, I definitely think that my influences and my work is a reaction against that smoothness. The Memphis group, back then, were also an influence. I admired their explosion of forms and their reassembling, of putting things together in such a way that the outcomes provided some freedom — which was also smooth in a way. And, of course, Ron Arad. Mostly his, what do you call it, the one-off series and his earlier work like the concrete stereo. Ron Arad has, in some ways, gotten smoother as the money and clients have come to him. But I think this smoothness is also because Arad works more with computers now and his forms are more computerised now.

I went to work for Ron Arad, you know, to get some work experience, and I also did a work placement with Danny Lane. He is a glass artist and architect. His work then was about very good craft, but I don't know what he is doing now. At the beginning I did glass. Comparing Danny Lane with Ron Arad — he also thought he was an artist. In the 1980s Arad and Lane were very close, but Arad went this way and Lane the other.

Tejo Remy

I think there is a big difference in the way designers look at craft in England and Holland. In a way, craft objects can be really nice and ornate, but with craft there are sometimes certain points where the emphasis is more on the concept — the concept of how you thought about the process. I don't know if the concept is stronger in terms of the Dutch approach or if there is more emphasis on the concept in Dutch design, but I think the UK draws different lines between craft and design.

I admire this approach of making things that you find through a kind of anti-consumerist behaviour. This is what I am trying to do.

Stiletto (Frank Schreiner), Consumer's Rest Chair, 1983

Ron Arad, Well Tempered Chair, 1986

The buildings of MVRDV. They are in the *SuperDutch* book. They did some work in Lisbon, and in Hanover — the different layers, yeah.

I also love a lot of Koolhaas' buildings. But in particular, I liked his work when he did not build anything. I think his work was better in the beginning when he thought a lot about buildings. The building was the theory — in some ways that was his greatest work. I think it had something to do with the way Koolhaas put things together, which was, in some ways, actually very awkward. I think Koolhaas has a real boldness — he is brash and butch, aggressive, not feminine!

I also love a lot of Koolhaas' buildings. But in particular, I liked his work when he did not build anything. I think his work was better in the beginning when he thought a lot about buildings.

Tejo Remy

products

I have to think about products. I am not sure that I have a product in mind. Mostly, I admire the thought behind a product — how it is conceived.... In many ways, at the end, the product itself does not matter. At the end it is the process, not the product, which is most interesting. I think, in a way, I like the Internet as a product because you can access things, all kinds of information. In a way that is one of the best products of the last century. But what I like most is that you can get information that always has this liberty. It affects us hugely.

> In many ways, at the end, the product itself does not matter. At the end it is the process, not the product, which is most interesting.

books

I have read some anti-consumerist stuff, but not properly. The book *No Logo* by Naomi Klein and *Adbusters* magazine are quite clever — they are a bit like *Fight Club,* but they use graphics and words, whereas in *Fight Club* they use bombs. I don't really read much — I am a retired pauper. I think the world has changed now. What amazes me is when you are on a train now the entire carriage is reading a different Harry Potter book. It is like an escape from computing. Everyone wants to escape from his or her day-to-day existence. They want to fly around on broomsticks. I have read Harry Potter — I want to escape.

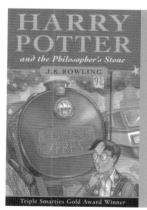

J K Rowling, Harry Potter and the Philosopher's Stone, book jacket, 1997

cars

I like cars. I like the Smart in a way. I think it's good. They are quite a
laugh to drive — they are fun. I also know this artist and designer
called Oskar de Kiefte who works on cars. He messes with cars so that
the back becomes the front, and the front becomes the back. He likes
to mess with the streamlined look of the car. I suppose his work can
be seen as similar to *Adbusters*. It is, perhaps, that sort of political
thing that they both do that I like.

Oskar de Kiefte,
The Converted Porche 924, 1995

Tejo Remy

George Lucas, Star Wars, promotional photograph, 1977

Cinema is maybe a little easier. When I have a chance, which I don't get a lot anymore, I watch kids movies with my children. But I also like them, of course. I have not yet gone to see *Harry Potter*.... I do like *Fight Club*, because I'm working with a colleague on an exhibition design and they have asked us to make a kind of furniture piece where people can sit and we are making a kind of product. A sort of digital screen where the pieces of art are behind it, and you come to approach the work like the scene in *Fight Club*....
There are a lot of directors and actors that are great, but it is difficult to pinpoint them. We can start from Hitchcock to the present day, and then with *Star Wars*. My problem with this is that you may be working on something and then you get influenced by what you see. So the most inspiring things to me are all of the things happening in the world right now. It depends on what you are working on and with.

I think you have to have a balance in your work between globalisation and locality. You have to make the most out of your environment, and locality is important to me. You have to pick up things on a day-to-day basis rather than merely accepting what is pumped into you. It is difficult to say explicitly "this is this" or "this is that", as you need everything when you design. In the beginning I did a lot more furniture — one-off pieces, you know. But now I go more and more towards making things for a certain place, a specific site. For example, the last project I made, for the Italian Foundation, was a kind of bar space. We used different levels, floor levels and spaces to sit at the end of the bar. The levels go from 30 centimetres to 120 centimetres. The furniture becomes more of an area, it becomes very architectural. This has dramatically changed how that environment works in terms of breaking the barriers down between furniture and interior space. It's the same difference. It is still furniture.

Tejo Remy

Tejo Remy

Vrom Canteen, 2004

Tejo Remy

artists

In terms of artists, I like this Dutch artist called Mik — Aernout Mik. He mostly makes videos — you have to see them, they are very disturbing. His work is more realistic than Matthew Barney's, for example. Matthew Barney's videos are more fantasy, but Mik's videos are much more realistic and more disturbing in that sense.

press

Magazines? I like the computer magazine *Mac*. I also enjoy *Frame*. *Wallpaper* I have read only once — it is very superficial. I usually just buy a collection of magazines and go through them, because they all have items that are interesting to me in one way or another. Newspapers? I read the newspaper *NRC*.

Tejo Remy

My work is mostly inspired by Nick Cave as far as music is concerned. The You Can't Lay Down Your Memories chest of drawers is named after a Nick Cave song. I also listen to music from Sesame Street at the moment — it is my daughter's favourite programme.

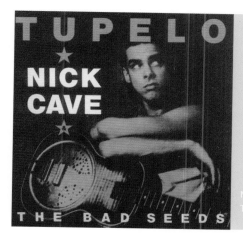

Nick Cave and the Bad Seeds, The Firstborn is Dead, CD cover, 1985

If I were having the dinner party of all time, I would invite the first caveman — prehistoric man. I would also have to invite my girlfriend — that is the diplomatic answer. I would also bring my daughter to the party.

Arnout Visser

Arnout Visser was born in 1962 and studied at the Art School in Arnhem, The Netherlands, from 1984 to 1989, and also at the Domus Academy in Milan, Italy. Visser works mainly as a freelance designer, but has had a close association with Droog Design since its inception in 1992. In 1997 Studio Arnout Visser was established. The Studio now acts as a base for Visser's diverse design activities, which include the use of diamond cutting tools, working with glass, and experimenting with liquid resins, wood and metal.

The ideas for Visser's designs are often initiated by physical or mechanical laws, such as Archimedes Hydrostatics Law. His products are often the logical results of his enquiries, such as his oil and vinegar bottle, Salad Sunrise, where the oil floats on the vinegar in this object as the oil is lighter than vinegar. Visser believes the immediate cause for a new product may vary but that products must continue to captivate the user. He feels that one should be committed to them, and they should inherently tempt you to touch them, to feel them and try them out. Visser prefers a sober use of colours, as he firmly believes the material already possesses a beauty of its own.

Arnout Visser has exhibited his work to an international audience and his products can be found in permanent collections around the world, including the Museum of Modern Art, New York, the Design Museum, London, and the Kunsthal, Rotterdam.

Real World Picture Reformer, 2001

There are designers, from several generations, of course, but let's start with Archimedes and with Leonardo da Vinci. Thanks to Archimedes' Laws I thought of a letter water-balance and, so, my product is called Archimedes. The letter water-balance started as an idea for using Archimedes' Law itself, and I developed several forms for it. I used models in wood, plastic and glass, developing the form solely on functional lines, and this was dictated by trying to get it running, to get it working. I have also got some excellent books about old machines that are also very inspirational to me. I bought some beautiful technical books while in Italy, along with some other excellent technical stuff in Milan. These books demonstrate things like the Morse Code system and how it works. You know, there is this kind of false starting point for a lot of products.

As for designers, I first studied here in Arnhem, and after that I went to the Domus Academy in Milan. One of the professors over there was Michele de Lucchi, an excellent guy. Another was Ingo Maurer. And, generally speaking, I like a lot of Italian design. And Andreas Branzi, of course. It was fortunate that Andreas Branzi was a teacher at Domus when I was there. He stimulated you not to think and to join the Italian way of design, but to develop your own way within an Italian school. This was a very good piece of advice — not to imitate but to somehow develop your own strategy. As I am now a teacher myself I, too, try to look for qualities in a person that tell of something of themselves. That is what is interesting, not how to make another clone of something, but how to find the spark within a person. That is what is exciting.

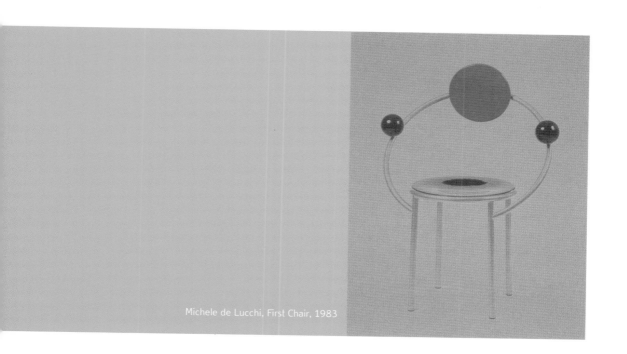

Michele de Lucchi, First Chair, 1983

Ingo Maurer, Birdie Chandelier, 2002

Yes, I like buildings and stuff, but for me there is an easy answer. Water towers. These used to be everywhere, and they were often quite beautiful. And I also like buildings that have a special purpose, like in Italy when families used to build enormous towers to impress each other. There is one particular tower near Tuscany with some heavy trees on its top, some old oak trees, real trees. It's a very interesting building. The town itself is called San Jimano, in Tuscany. I am dyslexic so I'm not really sure if that's right. I am afraid I might have got the name wrong. But that is the kind of building I admire. The kind of buildings that are always stimulating to me are hydropower machinery buildings, such as the big dykes in The Netherlands. These types of buildings interest me a lot. And Modern architecture can be exciting, especially when it integrates scientific or technical functions. For example, Norman Foster utilised a telescope system to get more daylight inside his Hong Kong and Shanghai Bank building. I think his use of the telescope system is very clever. The system concentrates light inside the building in a brilliant way. Of course, human light is the best light available, whereas sunlight *and* artificial light in buildings can be very problematic to get right. Also interesting for design, I think, is the development of enormous computer processing power. We like to use it, of course, but simple things are so much different. The human brain is different from the computer. For instance, it takes five times longer to read a page of text on a computer screen than it does on paper. Nobody can understand exactly why this is, but it is different. And, of course, there are millions of examples of products that have been designed by a computer mind as oppsed to a 'real' mind. It is important for us designers to react to that.

Arnout Visser

Foster and Partners, Hong Kong and Shanghai Banking
Corporation Headquarters, Hong Kong, 1979–1986

Garthamlock Water Towers, Glasgow

Arnout Visser

No real designed products, but maybe products like the bicycle. I think it is interesting to see that the bicycle has not changed much for over 100 years. Also, the toilet has not changed in 150 years, since the development of the swan neck system. You can still buy a toilet seat for a product that is 150 years old! And so, I like the kind of product that is difficult to improve upon. But on the other hand, of course, we as designers are always trying to do just that. For example, with the bicycle we are currently trying to develop a new machine, which, in theory, should work even more efficiently, but in practice it doesn't at all. The bicycle, as a system, is such a human invention, it works so well. I think this stays with us. And, of course, a bicycle looks so beautiful — that's the way you have to do it. But if you see the first 50 years of the bicycle's development, it starts with big wheels and stuff, and it takes time to come to the point we're at now. So, the bicycle is still a thing to work with and support, and a starting point for other products.

Arnout Visser

I like the kind of product that is difficult to improve upon. But on the other hand, of course, we as designers, are always trying to do just that.

Arnout Visser

Coco Cola Lamp, 2000

Glasservies Centraal Museum, 1999

Tegelkeuken, 2001

Icecube Insulation Bowl, 2002

books

I am reading a book about life in Africa. The book is called *The Dance of the Leopard*. It is by a Flemish writer called Lieve Joris. It is an interesting book, a documentary of changing powers there, and how this affects the peoples' way of life. It is interesting for me, as I am a kind of nervous guy, and when I was working in Africa things changed for the good for me. As a starting point, we say here, "We need this and we need that", but in Africa you say, "Well, we have this so what can we do?" It is completely the other way round. And from this we developed a series of products. For example, the sugar elephant — this was the kind of product that we started with — the things you saw, the sugar and milk, from which we made a drawing and were told, "Yeah, we can do that."

... a friend of mine bought a Land Rover, made in 1966, and it is very interesting to see now that some pieces of the car were made ten years before 1966 and some ten years after, but they can be mixed up. But I think there are no examples of truly inspirational cars nowadays.

Arnout Visser

A car, yes that's nice. A year ago, perhaps two years ago, I thought of an idea for a blow-up car. It was a car that is inflated with air, so inside you have a slightly heavier or higher atmosphere and the whole structure is made stable by the air. It is one big air sack really. And, so, I talked with someone, a guy at Fiat in Italy, and he said, "Excellent, this idea is perfect." But Fiat was changing at this time with new people, new deadlines and stuff and they kept on saying that they were very interested but they didn't do anything with the idea, so I don't know. Anyway, that was the idea, to develop a car using a new way of thinking — because you don't want much weight in a car. Weight is the big problem in car design. So, with this idea, we developed a blow-up car that would weigh about 450 kilos, which is about half the weight of a normal car. It's much better than existing cars. It would be safer and it would use less energy. But the idea was too advanced and too complicated — and it was a completely new way of thinking. On the other hand, this car will eventually come, but it will take some time. For myself, a friend of mine bought a Land Rover, made in 1966, and it is very interesting to see now that some pieces of the car were made ten years before 1966 and some ten years after, but they can be mixed up. But I think there are no examples of truly inspirational cars nowadays. Every year, I get a Citroën XM and every year all the pieces are developed slightly differently and no longer fit one another. So, I have a car accident and then I look for exactly the same model because it is like a kind of fishing net — it is kind of closed. That's what is completely wrong, and what makes it expensive, as well as complicated. Of course, the ultimate car is the Hummer, the American army car, which is 2.5 metres wide. It is enormous. It's a new kind of Jeep, I would say. And it's quite expensive. I like French cars, especially Citroëns, because of their excellent suspension systems. The air pressure system they use for their suspension is great — like when you have glass in your car and you don't want it damaged.

Hummer H2 Sports Utility Vehicle, 2003

Arnout Visser

For now, Peter Greenaway, all his movies are masterpieces. He somehow manages to work between making films and designing at the same time. He is the 'author' of some excellent museum exhibitions. For example, he had a nice exhibition in Milan recently, and I have seen several installations of his work. And so that's why I think he is a perfect guy. Because I lived in Italy for a while I, of course, love classic Italian films with all their strangeness, and with all the Baroque visual effects, like in Fellini. And as my brother is a filmmaker, I am quite interested in film. We try to make films here, as well, but we are amateurs in that sense, well tried amateurs I would say.

Peter Greenaway, all his movies are masterpieces. He somehow manages to work between making films and designing at the same time.

Arnout Visser

Pipilotti Rist. Do you know her? She is 26, 36 years old, she is a kind of nice video artist, and she is making beautiful videos of herself and her surroundings. But the interesting thing about her is that she keeps filming all the problems and difficulties in making her work and, how do you say, if something goes wrong during the filming or during the video editing, she incorporates this into the film itself. So you see a lot of 'snow' and things, mistakes, but these are used as a kind of decoration or style. I think this is very clever, using a system or series of problems that keep changing her design as she goes along. Pipilotti, she is from Sweden. No, she is a Swiss lady, a nice lady.

Also, artists like Panamarenko. He is an artist, and he makes sculptures, and he develops for example some... I have some books on him.... Panamarenko is a great guy, he is now 55 years old I think. He used to be an old hippie but with very nice 'physical' ideas. He develops, kind of, fantasy machines, poetic machines that go through space. And machines to fly and climb. One of his very first products, in 1964, was a pair of shoes with electro-magnets and two suckers on them so that you could walk on the roof, or on the ceiling. I saw an exhibition of his recently where he was developing some kind of animal dinosaurs that can fly into space by using the sun's energy. And he develops cars and stuff. They are always fantastic.

John Kormeling is another excellent artist. We have a video of his work here. John Kormeling also works with the car. Kormeling says the car is not the enemy, but somehow a friend. He is Dutch, living in Eindhoven. He has evolved some very nice ideas between form and design. He is developing a complete world from his own mind. He developed a big wheel which people can sit in and go round in circles. And he also developed one of these for cars, where you drive in with your car and you make a full circle. He has also developed architecture. He goes much further than normal artists, he has a story. And that makes him a good guy as well, by the way.

I subscribe and I am a member of a magazine called *Kijk* which translates as "the Look" in English. *Kijk* is a magazine for 12 year old boys. It is about how things work now and how they might work in the future. For the rest, I have magazines for my designer stuff, normal design magazines like *Form* and *Items*, which I like.

music

The Rolling Stones. That is because it is already 30 years or something since I first heard and liked The Rolling Stones. I am now 39, but my brother was nine years older than me, and he started to listen to pop music in 1962. I heard a lot of The Rolling Stones and I still like them.

The Rolling Stones, Flowers, CD cover, 1966–1967

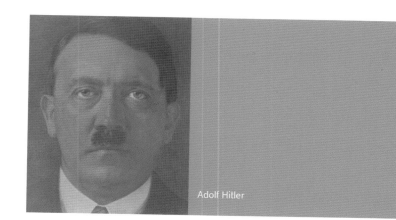
Adolf Hitler

If I were to have a dinner party, I would really like to have dinner with Leonardo da Vinci. Do you know da Vinci also made a drawing of a bicycle 500 years before the first bicycle was developed, but he didn't fully work it out. I think Leonardo and some other guys would be good. I would invite Adolf Hitler. I would ask him what was happening with him — we don't only have to have positive people. And since I am the son of a historian, I always take a historical view. My father was always talking about the Second World War and as I am quite interested in this period, as well, maybe there should be a little place for Adolf. I would also invite many artists. Panamarenko, for example. He's a great guy. And John Kormeling is an excellent guy, too. I would also ask Atelier van Lieshout. He is an interesting designer and artist and he is working in a group with a lot of Dutch artists who are doing experiential design and architecture. I like dinner, and when I was in Italy, Italian people made me feel very welcome. I was always surprised at the way Italian people made a party of every lunch and made a feast of every dinner. In Italy when you spend two hours preparing dinner it is quite normal — they take two hours to make spaghetti. That way of thinking is quite different from The Netherlands, because here it is difficult to find that kind of pleasure. I don't know what you are used to, but in The Netherlands dining is all very middle of the road, and the food is all middle of the road. It's a pity.

Marcel Wanders

Marcel Wanders was born in Boxtel, south of Amsterdam. He studied at the Academy of Arts in Arnhem and then worked mostly as a freelance designer before founding his first company Wanders Wonders, in 1995. Currently, Wanders is Art Director and resident guru of the pioneering design firm, Moooi, the Dutch word for beautiful. Wanders started the company to provide a haven for young designers who had challenging ideas that might otherwise have been ignored. At Moooi, he and other designers come up with unusual solutions to everyday objects. These are mainly household items that defy conventional ideas of beauty, such as his candle-shaped electric lamp, BLO, which turns itself off when you blow on it.

Major design brands, such as Italian furniture manufacturers Cappellini and Flos are snapping up Wanders' designs. Cappellini produces Wanders' most famous creation, the Knotted Chair, which he designed in 1995. The chair is made of a hand-knotted net of rope soaked in resin, and looks like macramé or a fishing net, but with a high-tech lightness and strength. The Museum of Modern Art, New York, and the San Francisco Museum of Art, among others, feature the Knotted Chair in their collections.

Gobi Bath Tub, 2001

I think there are a lot of designers I have learnt from. There are both artists and designers, but if I were to say who has had the most influence on my life, I would say it is more the big heroes like Jesus Christ and Nelson Mandela. These people are really role models for me. I don't necessarily follow in their footsteps, it's not like that. And also, for me as a designer, I think the lives of people in general have had an influence, rather than the specific work of designers from the past.

I try to develop myself in a broad sense. I don't want to be this big, deep designer. I try to be as superficial as possible. It sounds a bit strange, but I try to be very superficial because that will give me width instead of depth. I think artists should be deeply in touch with their own souls, but I think designers should not be as deep, so that they can touch a lot of people at the same time — on a less personal note, but on a real level, where they can either find some way through with their products, have fun with them. It cannot be that personal, otherwise it will never touch many people. So, I also like the thinking that I need to be superficial, not as a person, but as a designer. I'm a designer on one hand, but a businessman on the other. And I only try to work with companies that I fully respect, from a business and a personal point of view. It's important who they are as people *and* what they sell as a company.

But I guess, if I was talking from a design perspective, then the people who have inspired me are probably the same as those for other people, designers like Charles Eames, Philippe Starck, Antonio Gaudi and Issey Miyake — the big heroes, and some smaller heroes, too. I also like Frank Gehry. I think his work is fabulous, and he's one of my heroes. And there are also companies like Swatch, which are very inspirational to me, or have been. They are not so exciting at the moment, but tomorrow they could be very inspiring again.

Antonio Gaudi, La Sagrada Familia, 1882-1926

Frank Gehry, Cardboard Furniture, 1972

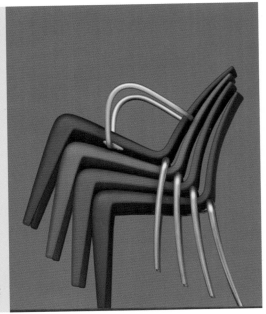

Philippe Starck, Louis XX Stacking Chair, 1992

Knotted Chair, 1995.

Marcel Wanders

Coffee Table, 2004

Flare, 2003

Whenever I go to Milan, I try to go to the Piazza del Duomo. It was my first contact with the design world as a design student, so it is kind of a landmark for me. It's like my first connection to the design world internationally.

I also admire the homes where I have lived in the south of Holland. And I really like this little church called Ronchamp. I was travelling and I was probably 20 years old. We were in the middle of Italy and we had seen some churches, most of which were very exciting. It is unbelievable what has been done in churches. They have always been a place of inspiration for me, theatres and churches, they go far beyond what has been built elsewhere. So, we had this trip to churches and we were so inspired by the strength and the creativity that people put into architecture hundreds of years ago for the sake of religion, for the sake of drama or for the sake of communicating to people thatthings were great.

And we were a little bit sad, in a way, because our time lacks this. I remember we drove back from Italy and we drove past Ronchamp and I said, "Isn't there something there?" So we went and came upon this beautiful church, which was made more or less now, and it was so good for us. It was the best thing that could have happened to us. All this energy came back to us. There is some great architecture at the moment. There's not just one, but a few architects who are doing great things, people like Rem Koolhaas and Frank Gehry. There is not just one piece of good architecture. There is a strong foundation of good architecture, a lot of which is made in Holland....

Le Corbusier, Notre Dame du Haut, Ronchamp, 1950/1954

Marcel Wanders

Swatch is not only a product. But what I like about Swatch is their knowledge of communication as a part of design, and not necessarily their knowledge of their product. In the end they make beautiful products, but I admire their thinking as a whole. I prefer wearing a Rolex watch to a Swatch because as a watch it says more than any Swatch. But a Swatch is a great product, and they have a great brand. And Swatch do great things with their products, like manufacture watches that give you access to football matches and museums and so on.

I enjoy so many things that I try not to mystify any of them. I try to enjoy most of them because I see things changing all the time and by making heroes of a few things you become fixed. It is very hard if you have this one product that you are excited about. So, I have this whole area of things I enjoy.

I remember one day I came across a Japanese habit. The Japanese catch a fish and they make a little hole in it to take out the intestines, then they fill it with rice wine, seal the hole, and hang it in the attic for a year or so. They then remove the head and drink the wine that has been infused with the fish, and they break off parts of the fish to eat with the wine. And the fish is crispy, with a strong fish taste and a taste of wine. I thought this to be a really inspiring idea, and one I try not to forget. But I try not to tell myself this is the best idea, or the best thing ever, because I know tomorrow that things will change and there will be something else that is even better. So, I try to enjoy and look at the world in different ways, and this way I enjoy a lot of things, not just one. I really look for the good in things and usually there is something.

I enjoy so many things that I try not to mystify any of them. I try to enjoy most of them because I see things changing all the time and by making heroes of a few things you become fixed. It is very hard if you have this one product that you are excited about. So, I have this whole area of things I enjoy.

The last book I read that I thought was great was a book by Ken Wilbur, *Surrender and Battle*. It's beautiful. It is about his wife dying of cancer and the process and the moments in-between, how he feels about certain moments. I tend to read more documentary stuff, more investigative books. I try to educate myself in areas I know little about, which could be the function of the brain or new ways of communication. Things I find interesting. Marketing strategy, branding, someone who has a new idea and how he or she comes about that. Books where there are new strategies about branding or marketing. Another book I read which was great was about archaeology. It was about the development of totally new ideas on the Darwin's theories. Things like how do people change over time and how does the brain work. I like to read new ideas about these sorts of subjects.

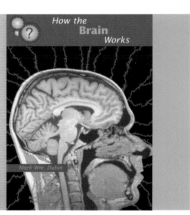
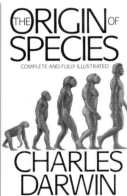

Mark Wm Dubin, How the Brain Works, book jacket, 2002

Charles Darwin, The Origin of Species, book jacket 1859

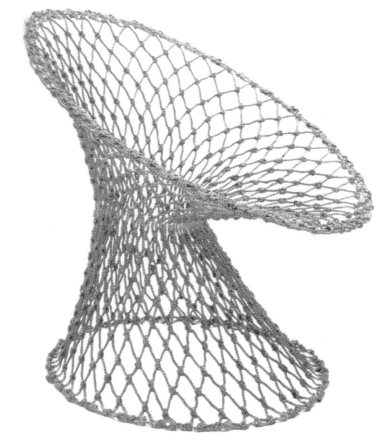

Fishnet Chair, 2001

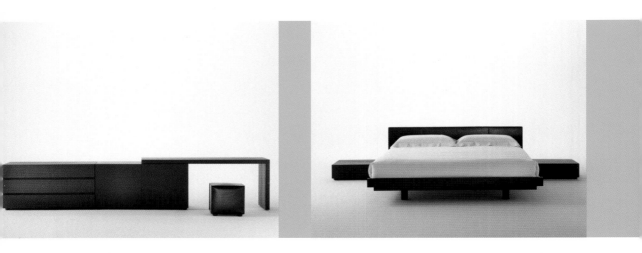

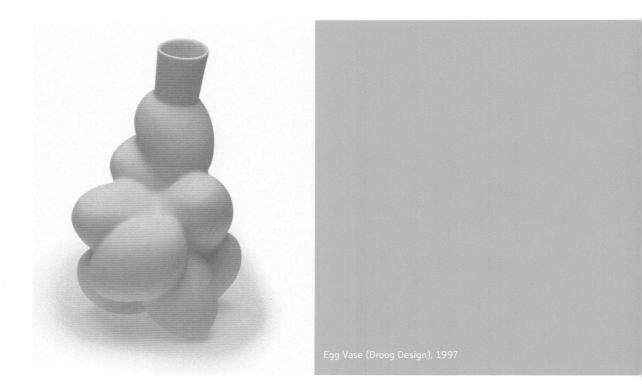

Egg Vase (Droog Design), 1997

Marcel Wanders

Sponge Vase (Droog Design), 1997

Carbon Chair, 2004

I like Porsche cars. Not the 911, but I like the Porsche 928. It's a beautiful car. Not the oldest model or the newest types... I like the Porsche 928s made around the late 80s, beginning of the 90s.

Porsche 928, c. 1988

I think *Rocky* is a first class movie. Every Friday at 5.30 we play *Rocky* and that for us is the end of the week. What I don't like so much about modern movies is that I can feel stupid at the end of the film, or I didn't enjoy myself or it was boring or I didn't feel happy. What I think makes a good movie — meaning it is probably a bad movie for other 'cultural' people — is, first, that I have enjoyed it and, second, that I have had fun or learnt something or got a good feeling from it. Generally, this type of film always starts with a person who is challenged, then has more problems, and then starts to solve the problems because he likes someone else, and, then, at the end, he enjoys himself. All the good movies to me are like that, because all films are about making heroes. There may be all kinds of stories, but this is how I want to see my life, and I want to see people do the same story, and I'd like to enjoy that, and be inspired by that. There are cultural stories, different ways to see this same storyline, and the good part is I understand a movie like that. I like it that way, simple.

This morning I was visiting two old artists. One was a teacher of mine. He told me he has been on the phone to his friend who is a photographer, and he has been bragging about me, telling this friend that I was an ex-student and am now a great designer. Anyway, this artist wants to show me something, so I go to meet him, and he is probably 70 years old, and he had this problem, and when my friend the teacher showed him my card case, it helped him solve his problem. So, he wanted to show me that his art was inspired by design — it's like the saying "art inspires design". But it's good to know that it also works the other way.

Art to me is very inspirational. We have an inspiration board in the studio where we throw everything that inspires us. Sometimes art is too boring for me when I hear lots of different stories and see nothing that is close to inspirational. And sometimes I get really sad about it and sometimes I see the most amazing details in great objects. So, I'm trying to think what art has been inspirational to me lately. What I have seen over the last years is not yet an art form to me. But if you write that some historic figure will pick up on it and say it is an art form. What I see in the arts is that something has been changing. If we were to go to a gallery in the 1950s we would have our hats just so and our chic clothing. We would visit this totally strange guy probably wearing a straw hat and non-polished shoes — someone who is a free man, someone who can do what he wants, is free to follow his heart. And if we were to buy a painting of his we would feel we were buying part of his freedom, we have a connection to him and therefore we feel more spiritual and free. I think this is a big part of the functionality of art — that it gives people a connection with freedom.

Then, given the same situation now, what I see more and more is that we go to the art galleries and we are wearing the straw hats and we are crazy, we are free. We have no strong connection to religion any more. We don't have strong relationships with our families. If we have a job, we know tomorrow we could have something else because we are free. We can do whatever we want today, and tomorrow, because we are free people. So, artists are not looking for freedom anymore, they are looking for the opposite. They are obsessed with one thing and they follow it, in the most stupid of ways. Like they get obsessed with one little shape, so they produce hundreds of them. And like a friend of mine who has started being a dog for a month. His girlfriend ties him up and walks him in the street, and if he pees he pees against a tree in the street. Art is getting so obsessed with little things. And in a way, what is the point of having freedom if we don't have anything important enough to invest it in? These artists find something to invest 100 per cent of their freedom in. 100 per cent devotion to one stupid little object. But to me that is really inspiring. The 100 per cent dedication I've seen in art is a new thing to me. There are probably designers who have the same approach, but it's not so strong visually, because the strength of art is direct and can be very powerful. A designer, however, is maybe working for a company who is not so dedicated, and they probably don't find a way. They have to find another type of public, or other ways. Whereas if an artist makes 100,000 bulbs and lays them out in a gallery, it is very clear he is a madman. And the same for the artist who makes squares out of the seeds of flowers. It is just incredible. I see this more and more and I say, "Why?" Because we are so free that we are lost also. And they are not lost, because they know where they have put their freedom. It may be somewhat stupid, but at least they know. I feel this is part of our culture at the moment. We like people who know what they want and are willing to die for it. We admire that and I think these artists do that.

I think Antony Gormley is one of those artists who makes all these little objects and puts them in a room... and Tony Cragg. I have a musician friend who is dedicating four years of his life to discovering the original sound of a parrot. You give yourself a stupid question and you will follow it and beautiful things will come of it because no one has done that before. And this is a beautiful idea because he will find new sounds to present to us. It's like Cragg or Gormley. They probably find some spiritual reason for it, but it is not the real thing. It's their fantasy of the real thing.

... artists are not looking for freedom any more, they are looking for the opposite. They are obsessed with one thing and they follow it, in the most stupid of ways. Like they get obsessed with one little shape, so they produce hundreds of them....

Marcel Wanders

We don't have subscriptions to any of the design or interior design magazines. I think we have one to *Frame*. Sometimes I buy one or two magazines and sometimes they are sent to us, so that is more or less what is there. I don't read anything regularly. I try not to see any journals or the news on TV, and I never read magazines! I think a newspaper is made up of 80 per cent bad news, and if I look at my life at least 80 per cent is good news, so I don't want to be misled by the real world because my real world is more interesting.

I try to be informed about the news that concerns me and that I am willing to react to, which means I get used to not reacting to really important stuff, which I don't like. If someone was to hit someone else in the street I will go there. But seeing people being killed on TV and not doing anything will not teach me to do the right thing. I can remember the time I decided not to watch TV, about five or six years ago in Yugoslavia. There was a bridge over a valley and a bomber heading for it, and we saw people running towards the bridge, and I didn't get it. Shouldn't you flee instead of going there? And the plane went to the bridge and didn't bomb it because of the people and the cameras everywhere. That would never have happened 20 years ago, and I realised the only reason it wasn't bombed was because I was one of the people watching the bridge. And partly I was happy, but I was also unhappy because I felt I was being used as a weapon in a battle I knew nothing about. Looking at the TV is OK, but creating an opinion based on that, which we all do, is becoming a weapon and you are being manipulated. So, I decided not to be misused again, and if I watch TV now I try not to have an opinion on it.

> I think a newspaper is made up of 80 per cent bad news, and if I look at my life at least 80 per cent is good news, so I don't want to be misled by the real world because my real world is more interesting.

About six years ago I started to be really fond of the music you hear in large warehouses. Music is always there, but you never listen to it. I feel a lot of the new-age music is like this, and I like that. I like George Michael when I'm driving in my car. I have great fun singing along to him. I really like dance music, the fast kind. Not in the morning, but at the right moment I just adore it. I sometimes like Craig David, the voice of Anastasia, and Jamiroquai, but tomorrow it will be someone else. Then I like Fauré. I would die to have his requiem sung for me. I would probably have to. Music, and little sounds, can be very important to me. One of the most beautiful sounds I know I hear sometimes at one am where we live on the canal. It is not a normal canal, because it has really big ships crossing it, and you think, "Oh my God, that's in my studio." The ships can be as large as twice the height of the house and sometimes at night they have a bridge over the canal that has to open. And the ships collect there at night so they can pass the bridge together, and at times there can be about 15 ships waiting for the gate to open and there is hardly any noise and it is really beautiful. It's not music, but what is beautiful is that there is hardly any noise.

If you ask me what the three most beautiful things are in life, I would say music and dancing, and the third is love. To me these are the three best parts of life. What would be first, music or dancing, I don't know. Is it dancing on its own or is it the reaction to the music? This whole area is so great to me.

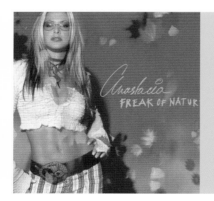

Anastacia, Freak of Nature,
CD cover, 2001

Jamiroquai, A funk odyssey,
CD cover, 2001

Pablo Picasso

Nelson Mandela

people

If I was to say who has had the most influence on my life and who my heroes are, then it has to be Jesus Christ and Nelson Mandela, as I have already mentioned. These people stand out. They have a big chance and really go for it knowing that they are not doing it for themselves but for a greater good. These people are really role models for me. I don't necessarily follow in their footsteps. It's not like that, but that for my life they are more inspiring than a designer who makes a beautiful object, which is very inspiring for me also, for me as a person.

You know, I try to have a lot of humans that I admire, not just one. It's just like influential designers. There are so many of them who for so many different reasons are really great people. Then there are really great people who have done some really terrible things, but who are still my heroes, even though I know they have done bad things. If I look at myself I have done some good things, but I have also done some terrible things. And I try to better myself. I'm not going to feel bad about who I am just because I have a few weak spots. I'm not going to beat myself up because I am not perfect at the moment. But, you know, people like Picasso — a great person, an absolutely stunning creative person, but also terrible. He would be the last one that you would want to call your father. What I would like to grow to be is a person who is great in all parts of his life. Not only the great artist, not only the great designer, not only the money machine, not only the great father, but I'd like to do the whole thing. This will probably cost me in one area, but I don't just want to be great in one area. I want to be absolutely great in all areas. If I look at people like Picasso, I see this guy who looks pretty good, but has a heart this big and its pumping so hard that it explodes, and then there's another guy with a dick this big that is bumping along the floor. It's like people not growing in a balanced way. To me that is the biggest challenge, to grow in balance. To be a greater person and not be malformed by being great. That's the challenge. It's difficult, but that's the challenge for me.

Tokujin Yoshioka

Tokujin Yoshioka was born in Japan in 1967 before going on to
study at the Tokujin Yoshioka was born in Japan in 1967.
Following studies at the Kuwasawa Design School he worked
for the late furniture and interior designer Shiro Kuramata. In
1988 he joined the Miyake Design Studio, and was subsequently
promoted to manage and design all Issey Miyake retail outlets.
In 1992 he started to work freelance and in 2000 established his
own studio, Tokujin Yoshioka Design.

Tokujin has been the recipient of many design awards including
the Award of Excellence by JDC Design, and the 2001 ID Annual
Design Review Award. He has since recieved the A&W Award,
Designer for the Future, and the Mainichi Design Award.

His internationally recognised Honey-Pop paper furniture is in the
permanent collection at the Vitra Design Museum and the Pompidou
Centre, Paris.

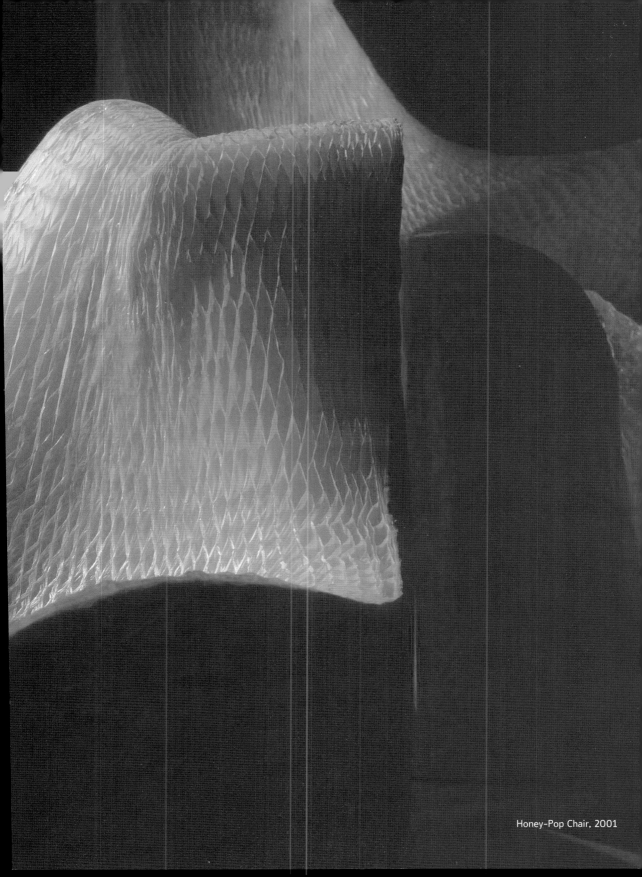

Honey-Pop Chair, 2001

The main inspiration for me has been Issey Miyake. I have been inspired by Miyake's innovative attitude toward challenging new things. Maybe this is because Miyake taught me when I was younger, but generally speaking I admire individuals who can think in a different way than I do. I do not have any other designers, in particular, in mind. Miyake was my teacher and I worked for him, so he is the single greatest influence on my life and my work. Shiro Kuramata has also inspired me and I think I learned design through them.

I think the main reason for this is that Issey Miyake has an approach whereby he accepts various attitudes. It is the attitude behind an idea that Miyake thinks is most important. It is not the form that matters the most, but the thought behind a design. In other words, it is the design process, the way that a designer works through a project that is important. This is what I really admire about Miyake.

For me, I want to do something which no one has ever done before, and that is not to design with design, not to take a source from design, but to take everything from other sources and to do something different. I know how difficult it is to make things, to create things, so I could never think about merely copying someone else's work and changing it a little bit here or there to make a design. I do not want to do that.

I think I get more influences from the worlds of art and cinema than from the design world. What would I like to do? I would like to do anything, anything at all. I would like to do something that I have never seen before. I intend to challenge at least one new thing, which would ultimately create new values that might lead to the future. I would love to work with NASA. I would like to work on any project with them. I think these are the things that excite, amaze, surprise, move people, to see those things. I would like to do something close to that, something like that. I want to make the impossible possible. These are the things that truly move people.

buildings

The Eiffel Tower in Paris is one of the most inspiring landmarks. It is not that I feel that the architectural features matter most, but that I am influenced by the atmosphere when I go near the Eiffel Tower. I also love the Duomo in Milan. I feel there is something really outstanding in these two buildings, because back when they were constructed they lacked a lot of the technology that we have today.

I do not know what it is about the atmosphere in the Eiffel Tower. It is the feeling when one goes into the tower. Maybe it's the air, or the atmosphere up there. It's more or less the same feeling at the Duomo in Milan.

I believe modern architecture is a sort of culture. It is sort of like the establishments you get for writers. When I was a student, however, I went to The Arab World Institute in Paris, by Jean Nouvel. This was about 15 years ago. I really admired the way the clockwork mechanisms opened and closed on the windows.

Gustav Eiffel, Eiffel Tower,
Paris 1889

Jean Nouvel, L'Institut du Monde
Arabe, Paris, 1987-1988

MUJI Infill Renovation, 2003

Tokujin Yoshioka

A-POC Shop Interior Design, 2001.

Hermes, "Air Du Temps", 2004

And Kiss Me Goodbye, 2004

There are so many great products that I cannot decide on any specific ones. There is really nothing in particular, but I do like cars, generally speaking. I do not like superficial design that would be just there for profit or for the popularity. I cannot remember the names of any particular products as there are so many. What interests me is design outcomes that are born of reason. For instance, the form of cars is a result of their functions.

For example, I have a nice watch but I do not think that it is a classic design. I like the fact that it is not designed by a 'named' designer, it just functions well. I also like the fact that it is just a result of 'nature', and it is really 'natural'. The car I am driving right now is another example of a product that I think has developed naturally. The Mercedes Jeep I have is really natural.

I think that there should not be too much functionality in designed products. It is often really unnecessary. I like products that do not have 'designers' involved in the process of their being designed. I admire everyday products, products that are anonymous. Products that do not carry the 'signature' of their designer.

> I like products that do not have 'designers' involved in the process of their being designed. I admire everyday products, products that are anonymous. Products that do not carry the 'signature' of their designer.

Tokujin Yoshioka

books

I do not have any particular books or authors in mind. I don't read very many books.

cars

The car I drive just now I love. It is a Mercedes Benz Jeep. I also find the Smart an inspiration. And Ferrari cars are beautiful. I do not know very much about Ferrari, but I recently went to an exhibition of Ferrari cars — models and prototypes... I just wanted to look at them all day. The structure of a Ferrari is so beautiful.

The Enzo Ferrari, 2002

It is not that I go to see a movie looking for inspiration, but I think the unreality that I see in movies inspires me. I can watch just about every sort of movie, except horror movies. I also love the actor Matt Damon, but I don't really know why. I guess if I were pushed to give my favourite Matt Damon movie then I would say *Le Grand Bleu* — a diving movie that was directed by Luc Besson. But I like most of Matt Damon's movies. I have so many favourite movies, though. I don't know. I recently watched some of Kurosawa's films, and I found them very similar to my work. I especially admire his *Seven Samurai* and *Yume*.

Akira Kurosawa, Seven Samurai,
promotional postcard, 1954

Tokujin Yoshioka

I love art. It is fairly obvious that there are a lot of influences that I use in my work. The fields of reference that I tend to use originate more from the art world than the design world. Really, I am not interested in the design world very much. I am much more interested in how the atmosphere of things change. So, for me, it is not really that important how the design world views my work. I simply do not care. The design world tends to distinguish a genre, like the category of 'nice things'. Even between design and art, they want to separate these two things. But I think it doesn't matter. I don't feel, or understand, the need to categorise things. It is much more important if the product or service is needed by the society — or not. I once worked with both Tim Hawkinson and Anish Kapoor, and I admire both of them as artists. I think it might be because they don't make things beautiful, but they do make things perfect without making them beautiful. I am also a great admirer of Rebecca Horn's work and recently I saw a Richard Wilson exhibition that I loved enormously.

The fields of reference that I tend to use originate more from the art world than the design world. Really, I am not interested in the design world very much. I am much more interested in how the atmosphere of things change.

I do not subscribe to any magazines. The publishers send some to me. I receive *Domus*, and I keep most of them. I scan particular pieces in a magazine. I especially like the pages in *Domus* that show the process of making things. I also receive *Interni* and *Abitare*. *Interni* were here just recently. They came to interview me. I also read the Japanese newspaper *Asahi* on a daily basis. I love getting the news, particularly World Business Satellite. I watch the news, or documentary programmes, in the evening when I get home.

A-POC Making Issey Miyake
and Dai Fujiwara Installation,
2001

Tokujin Yoshioka

Metamorphose — Wind of
LED, Peugeot, 2004

Audi Showroom
Concept Proposal, 2001

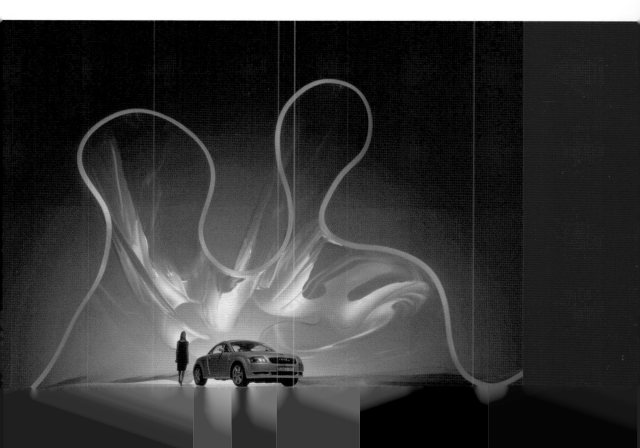

I do not have any musical influences, none at all. I think what influences me most in my design work tends to be technology. Chemistry and technology probably influence my work most. For instance, I recently looked at binocular lens technology for street furniture and extruded glass for seating to almost one metre thick. I like things that are not born from design. The aim is not to design from design, but to draw upon inspirations and reference sources from other areas. I am always exploring the latest scientific and technological advances. For example, at the moment I am working on seating made out of paper. I keep up to date by continually asking questions. It is not the same all the time, it's different questions for each project depending on what I'm working on. I am really interested in the way things change.

Chemistry and technology probably influence my work most. For instance, I recently looked at binocular lens technology for street furniture, and extruded glass for seating to almost one metre thick. I like things that are not born from design.

Tokujin Yoshioka

people

Leonardo da Vinci. I admire the imagination that he had in his work.
Issey Miyake. He has been the single most important influence on my
life and work. If I were to have a dinner party I do not really know who
I would like to invite. I have never really thought about anything like
that before.

Leonardo da Vinci

acknowledgements

This book has been a massive project in many, many ways. This means that there are a large number of people who deserve recognition for their support and advice. First, I wish to thank all the designers who feature in this book for their valuable time, extraordinary patience and willingness. I am especially grateful to all the designers for their responsiveness in sending me wonderful images of their work and their biographical details — usually at very short notice. Massive thanks are also due to the many companies and individuals that have donated wonderful images of their work for inclusion in the book.

I would also like to acknowledge the very generous financial support of the School of Design and Media Arts at Napier University. Without their backing the project would never have started. I would also like to thank the Carnegie Trust for their very kind financial backing. I would like to thank all the staff and students within the School of Design and Media Arts over the last couple of years for their understanding — particularly when my time has been short due to my commitments on this book. In particular I would like to thank Euan Winton whose help with the early book design layouts were invaluable. Catherine Harland, Anna McManus, Lorna Bruce and Maggie Spalding for their help with transcribing. I also wish to acknowledge the support of my colleagues Ed Hollis, Alex Milton, Duncan Hepburn, Bjorn Rodnes, Matthew Turner, Huw Davies, Megan Strickfaden, Ian Lambert, Will Titley, Jim Goodlet, Helen McCue, Annie Ross, Rob Walker, Jim Doig, Alex McLaren, Shona Richardson and Janet Abbott. I am sorry if I have forgotten to mention anyone by name — but you know you helped and I am very grateful — thank you!

I also wish to thank all at Black Dog Publishing for their help and co-operation during the project.

Last, but by no means least, I would like to dedicate this book to Alison and Charlie. Their love, support, and understanding has been unfaltering throughout.

Ron Arad

Ron Arad, Big Easy Chair, 1988, courtesy of Ron Arad Studio
Thomas Heatherwick, Sitooterie, Northumberland, 2000, courtesy of Thomas Heatherwick Studio
Jean Prouvé, Standard Chair, 1934, courtesy of Vitra AG, photo Hans Hansen
Charles and Ray Eames, Lounge Chair, 1956, courtesy of Vitra AG, photo Hans Hansen
Ron Arad, Rover Chair, 1981, courtesy of Ron Arad Studio
Ron Arad, Rolling Volume Armchair, 1989, courtesy of Ron Arad Studio
Ron Arad, After Spring Rocking Daybed, 1992, courtesy of Ron Arad Studio
Ron Arad, Bookworm Shelving System, 1994, courtesy of Ron Arad Studio
Le Corbusier, Notre Dame du Haut, Ronchamp, France, 1950-1955, courtesy of Jeffery Howe, © Jeffery Howe
Ron Arad, Oh Void, 2004, courtesy of Ron Arad Studio
Ron Arad, Lo-Rez-Dolores Table, 2004, courtesy of Ron Arad Studio
Citroën DS, c. 1967, courtesy of Anne-Marie Michel, © Citroën Communication
Anwar Sadat © The Guardian
Clare Short MP © The Guardian
Terry Jones © The Guardian
Mo Mowlam MP © The Guardian

Shin and Tomoko Azumi

Shin and Tomoko Azumi, Wireframe Reversible Bench, 1998, courtesy of Shin and Tomko Azumi
Achille and Pier Giacomo Castiglioni, Sella Stool, 1957, courtesy of Vitra Design Museum, © Vitra Design Museum, Weil am Rhein
Le Corbusier, Villa Savoye, Poissy-sur-Seine, 1929-1930, courtesy of Jeffery Howe, © Jeffery Howe
Chopsticks © DaMA, Napier University
Sony Walkman, c. 1995, © DaMA, Napier University
Shin and Tomoko Azumi, Lem Bar Stool, 2000, courtesy of Shin and Tomoko Azumi
Shin and Tomoko Azumi, HM30 Sofa, 2001, courtesy of Shin and Tomoko Azumi
Shin and Tomoko Azumi, Donkey 3, 2003, courtesy of Shin and Tomoko Azumi
Comb Chair, 2004, courtesy of Shin and Tomoko Azumi
Shin and Tomoko Azumi, Ship Shape, 2003, courtesy of Shin and Tomoko Azumi
Shin and Tomoko Azumi, Big Arm, 2000, courtesy of Shin and Tomoko Azumi
Shin and Tomoko Azumi, Orbital workstation, 2003, courtesy of Shin and Tomoko Azumi
Shin and Tomoko Azumi, Z A Angle, 2004, courtesy of Shin and Tomoko Azumi

Ronan and Erwan Bouroullec

Ronan and Erwan Bouroullec, Lit Clos Bed, 2000, courtesy of Ronan and Erwan Bouroullec
Achile and Pier Giacomo Castiglioni, Mezzadro, 1957, courtesy of Vitra Design Museum, © Vitra Design Museum, Weil am Rhein
Enzo Mari, Box Chair, 1975-1976, courtesy of Vitra Design Museum, © Vitra Design Museum, Weil am Rhein
Ronan and Erwan Bouroullec, Algue, 2004, courtesy of Ronan and Erwan Bouroullec
Ronan and Erwan Bouroullec, Assemblage, 2004, courtesy of Ronan and Erwan Bouroullec
Ronan and Erwan Bouroullec, Algue, 2004, courtesy of Ronan and Erwan Bouroullec
Ronan and Erwan Bouroullec, BETC, 2002, courtesy of Ronan and Erwan Bouroullec
Tokyo Streetscape, 2002, © Paul Rodgers
Ronan and Erwan Bouroullec, Untitled, courtesy of Ronan and Erwan Bouroullec
Ronan and Erwan Bouroullec, BETC, 2002, courtesy of Ronan and Erwan Bouroullec
Ronan and Erwan Bouroullec, Cabane, 2001, courtesy of Ronan and Erwan Bouroullec
Ronan and Erwan Bouroullec, TV Vase, 2001, courtesy of Ronan and Erwan Bouroullec
Citroën Mehari, c. 1970, courtesy of Anne-Marie Michel, © Citroën Communication
Malcolm Morley, Blue Burka, 2002
Gerhard Richter, Colour Fields, 1973

Matalı Crasset

Matali Crasset, Oritapi Carpet Game, 1999, courtesy of Matali Crasset

Joe Columbo, Tube Chair, 1969-1970, courtesy of Vitra Design Museum, © Vitra Design Museum, Weil am Rhein

Matali Crasset, Mobiwork Workspace, 2001, courtesy of Matali Crasset

Matali Crasset, Bath, HI hotel, 2003, Aquamass-Bruxelles, photo Aquamass

Matali Crasset, Happy Bar, HI hotel, NIce, photo Uwe Spoeting

Hella Jongerius, My Soft Office-Bed in Business for MOMA Workshperes Exhibition, 2000, courtesy of Hella Jongerius, © JongeriusLab

Matali Crasset, "Premis de construire", 2000, courtesy of Matali Crasset

Matali Crasset, Don-O, portable radio-cassette, 1995, courtesy of Matali Crasset

Matali Crasset, Teo Snoozing Stool, 1998, courtesy of Matali Crasset

Nick Crosbıe

Nick Crosbie, Birdhouse, courtesy of Nick Crosbie

Charles and Ray Eames, La Chaise, 1948, courtesy of Charles and Ray Eames

Nick Crosbie, Office in a Bucket, 2003, courtesy of Nick Crosbie

Nick Crosbie, Inflatable Table Light, courtesy of Nick Crosbie

Nick Crosbie, Fruit Bowl, courtesy of Nick Crosbie

Nick Crosbie, Mr and Mrs Prickly Salt and Pepper, courtesy of Nick Crosbie

Foster and Partners, City Hall, London, 1998-2002, courtesy of Foster and Partners, photo Nigel Young

Verner Panton, Pantower, 1968-1969, courtesy of Vitra Design Museum, © Vitra Design Museum, Weil am Rhein

Peter van der Jagt, Bottoms Up Doorbell, 1994, courtesy of Alex Milton, © Alex Milton

Lamborghini Miura P4005, 1969, courtesy of Alex Milton, © Alex Milton

Volkswagen Beetle, c. 1981, courtesy of Alexis Nicholson, © Alexis Nicholson

Nick Crosbie, Plug and Play amp speakers, 2003, courtesy of Nick Crosbie

Nick Crosbie, BMW, Air Camper, 2004, courtesy of Nick Crosbie

Motorola, 'Why Moto' campaign, 2004, courtesy of Nick Crosbie

Nick Crosbie, Big M, courtesy of Nick Crosbie

Henry VIII, 1491-1547, courtesy of The Bridgeman Art Library, collection of Belvoir Castle, Leicestershire

Prime Minister Tony Blair © The Guardian

Yasser Arafat © The Guardian

President George Bush © The Guardian

DumOffice

Dumoffice, Baby Unkle Easy Chair, 2000, courtesy of DUMoffice

Gaetano Pesce, 543 Broadway Chair, 1992, courtesy of Vitra Design Museum, © Vitra Design Museum, Weil am Rhein

Tokyo Streetscape, 2002, © Paul Rodgers

UPS Van Delivery, courtesy UPS, © 2004, United Parcel Service of America, Inc. All rights reserved

Dumoffice, Premsela Design Foundation Office, Amsterdam, 2003 courtesy of DUMoffice

Dumoffice, Azam Optician Store, The Hague, 2002 courtesy of DUMoffice

Dumoffice, Solarcity Lounge 100% Design, Rotterdam, 2003, courtesy of DUMoffice

Dumoffice, Baby Unkle Easy Chair for Kids, 2002, courtesy of DUMoffice

Rally Car, c. 2000, courtesy of Alex Milton, © Alex Milton

Stephen Fry © The Guardian

Freddie Mercury, 1946-1991, © The Guardian

Ian Hislop © The Guardian

Mark Dytham, KDa

Klein Dytham Architects, Leaf Chapel, 2004, photo © Katsuhisa Kida
Shiro Kuramata, How High the Moon Chair, 1986, courtesy of Vitra AG, photo Hans Hansen
Foster and Partners, Hong Kong and Shanghai Banking Corp. HQ, Hong Kong, 1979-1986, courtesy of Foster and Partners, photo Ian Lambot
Klein Dytham Architects, Undercover Lab, 2001, courtesy of Klein Dytham Architects
Klein Dytham Architects, Idee Workstation Furniture Showroom, 1996, courtesy of Klein Dytham Architects
Klein Dytham Architects, Beacon Advertising Agency Interior, 2002, courtesy of Klein Dytham Architects
Lucky Strike cigarette pack, Raymond Loewy, 1941
Aston Martin, c. 1960, courtesy of Alex Milton, © Alex Milton
Land Rover Range Rover, 2003, courtesy of Simon Fox, Autocar magazine
Museum Cafe, Tokyo, 2003, courtesy of Klein Dytham Architects
Klein Dytham Architects, Leaf Chapel, 2004, photo © Katsuhisa Kida
Klein Dytham Architects, Bloomberg ICE, photo © Katsuhisa Kida
Klein Dytham Architects, Pika Pika Pretzel temporary hoarding, 1999, courtesy of Klein Dytham Architects
Sir Winston Churchill 1874-1965, © The Guardian
Pope John Paul II © The Guardian

Martí Guixé

Martí Guixé, Galeria h2o Chair, 1998, courtesy of Ana Planella, Galeria H2O
Ettore Sottsass (Memphis School), Teodora Chair, 1986-1987, courtesy of Vitra AG, photo Hans Hansen
Plattenbau Socialist Architecture, c. 1950, © The Guardian
Tattoo, courtesy of Henry Hate, Prick London
Personal Computer © Paul Rodgers
Martí Guixé, PVC Bath Curtain, 2002, courtesy of The Original Cha-Cha S.L.
Martí Guixé, Home Aprons, 2001, courtesy of Martí Guixé
Martí Guixé, Plant Me Pets, 2003, courtesy of The Original Cha-Cha S.L.
Martí Guixé, Flamp, 1998, courtesy of Martí Guixé
Tokyo Taxi, 2002, © Paul Rodgers
Thomas Hirschhorn, Unfinished Walls, 2004, courtesy of Stephen Friedman Gallery, London, photo Stephen White
Queen Elizabeth II © The Guardian

Thomas Heatherwick

Thomas Heatherwick Studio, Plank Folding Coffee Table, 2001, courtesy of Thomas Heatherwick Studio
Thomas Heatherwick Studio, Hate Seat, courtesy of Thomas Heatherwick Studio
Santiago Calatrava, Milwaukee Art Museum Bridge, 2003, courtesy of the Milwaukee Art Museum, photo Timothy Hursley
Daniel Libeskind, Jewish Museum, Berlin, 1998, © Maggie Spalding
Thomas Heatherwick Studio, Harvey Nichols Autumn Intrusion, London, 1997, courtesy of Thomas Heatherwick Studio
Japanese temple, Kagoshima, Japan, 2003, photo Steven Speller
Thomas Heatherwick Studio, Blue Carpet Urban Square, Newcastle Upon Thames, 2002, courtesy of Thomas Heatherwick Studio
Pyramid teabags, 2004, © Paul Rodgers
Pop Tarts, 2004, courtesy of DaMA, Napier University
Citroën 2CV, c. 1950, courtesy of Anne-Marie Michel, © Citroën Communication
Citroën DS, c. 1955, courtesy of Anne-Marie Michel, © Citroën Communication
Thomas Heatherwick, Rolling Bridge, 2004, courtesy of Thomas Heatherwick Studio
Thomas Heatherwick Studio, B of the Bang Sculpture, Manchester, 2004, courtesy of Thomas Heatherwick Studio
Thomas Heatherwick Studio, Sitooterie, Northumberland, 2000, courtesy of Thomas Heatherwick Studio
Thomas Heatherwick Studio, Materials House, Science Museum, London, 1999, courtesy of Thomas Heatherwick Studio
Buckminster Fuller, 1895-1983, courtesy of the estate of R Buckminster Fuller

Scott Henderson

Scott Henderson, WOVO salad servers, 2001, courtesy of Scott Henderson, Smart Design
Pierre Paulin, Tongue model no. 577, 1967, courtesy of Vitra Design Museum, © Vitra Design Museum, Weil am Rhein
Philippe Starck, W W Stool, 1990, courtesy of Vitra AG, photo Hans Hansen
Charles and Ray Eames, LCW (Lounge Chair Wood), 1945, courtesy of Vitra AG, photo Hans Hansen
Scott Henderson, WOVO Chip and Dip Bowls, 2001, courtesy of Scott Henderson, Smart Design
Scott Henderson, WOVO Ice Bucket, 2001, courtesy of Scott Henderson, Smart Design
Scott Henderson, WOVO Bowl, 2001, courtesy of Scott Henderson, Smart Design
Scott Henderson, OXO Suction Cup Large Soap Dish, 2001, courtesy of Scott Henderson, Smart Design
Philippe Starck, Juicy Salif Lemon Squeezer, 1990, © Paul Rodgers
Maserati, GranSport, 2004, courtesy of courtesy of Simon Fox, Autocar magazine
Porsche 911 Turbo, 2004, courtesy of Ellie Gray, Porsche (UK), © Porsche AG
Scott Henderson, WOVO Thermal Carafe, 2001 courtesy of Scott Henderson, Smart Design
Scott Henderson, Orange ojex juicer 2000, courtesy of Scott Henderson, Smart Design
Scott Henderson, XM SkyFi Satellite Radio, 2002, courtesy of Scott Henderson, Smart Design
Scott Henderson, Alps game controller, 1997, courtesy of Scott Henderson, Smart Design

Ichiro Iwasaki

Ichiro Iwasaki, Mutech Music Centre (prototype), 2000, courtesy of Ichiro Iwasaki Design Studio, photo Hiromasa Gamo
Mario Bellini, Cab chair, model no. 412, 1976, courtesy of Vitra Design Museum, © Vitra Design Museum, Weil am Rhein
Stefano Giovannoni, Lilliput Salt and Pepper set, 1993, © Paul Rodgers
Stefano Giovannoni, Merdolino Toilet Brush, 1993, © Paul Rodgers
Bang and Olufsen Beomaster 6000, 1976, courtesy of www.BeoWorld.co.uk
Sigvard Bernadotte, Bang and Olufsen BeoCord Correct Stereo, 1960, courtesy of www.BeoWorld.co.uk
Ichiro Iwasaki, Espresso maker, Contrast 2003, courtesy of Ichiro Iwasaki Design Studio
Ichiro Iwasaki, RICOH, digital camera (prototype), 2004
Ichiro Iwasaki, Mutech Mini Component System, 2000, courtesy of Ichiro Iwasaki Design Studio, photo Hiromasa Gamo
Porsche Carrera GT, 2004, courtesy of Ellie Gray, Porsche (UK), © Porsche AG
Ichiro Iwasaki, Elecom PC table, 2000, courtesy of Ichiro Iwasaki Design Studio, photo Hiromasa Gamo
Ichiro Iwasaki, Teapot Contrast, 2003, courtesy of Ichiro Iwasaki Design Studio
Ichiro Iwasaki, Mutech Telephone with Answering Machine, 2000, courtesy of Ichiro Iwasaki Design Studio, photo Hiromasa Gamo
Katsura Funakoshi, Number of words arrived, 1991

Hella Jongerius

Hella Jongerius, Delft Blue B-Set, 2001, courtesy of Hella Jongerius, © JongeriusLab
Delftware, c. 1660, courtesy of Royal Delft, www.royaldelft.com
Factory Interior, c. 2000, © The Guardian
Herzog and de Meuron, Tate Modern, London, 1995-2000, © The Guardian
Hella Jongerius, Felt Stool, 2000, courtesy of Hella Jongerius, © JongeriusLab
Hella Jongerius, Maharam 'Repeat': Dots, 2001, courtesy of Hella Jongerius, © JongeriusLab
Hella Jongerius, Embroidered Tablecloth, 2000, courtesy of Hella Jongerius, © JongeriusLab
Hella Jongerius, Long Neck and Groove Bottle, 2000, courtesy of Hella Jongerius, © JongeriusLab
Hella Jongerius, Element from exhibition, 'Repeat' 2002, courtesy of Hella Jongerius, © JongeriusLab
Mercedes CLK Class Coupe, c. 2003, courtesy of Simon Fox, Autocar magazine
Wim Delvoye, Caterpillar, scale, Model No 4. 2002
Hella Jongerius, Pushed Washtub, 1996, courtesy of Hella Jongerius, © JongeriusLab
Hella Jongerius, Blizzard Bulbs, 2002, courtesy of Hella Jongerius, © JongeriusLab
Hella Jongerius, Kasese Sheep Chair, 1999, courtesy of Hella Jongerius, © JongeriusLab

RADI designers

RADI Designers, Fabulation Installation, Foundation Cartier pour l'Art Contemporain, Paris, 1999, courtesy of RADI Designers
Alessandro Mendini, Proust's Armchair, 1978, courtesy of Vitra Design Museum, © Vitra Design Museum, Weil am Rhein
Renzo Piano Building Workshop, Tjibaou Cultural Center, New Caledonia, 1991-1998, courtesy of Renzo Piano Building Workshop, photo John Gollings
Frank O Gehry, Wiggle furniture, 1972, courtesy of Vitra AG, photo Hans Hansen
Citroën 2CV, c. 1980, courtesy of Anne-Marie Michel, © Citroën Communication
Volkswagen Beetle, c. 1980, © Alexis Nicholson
RADI Designers, Whippet Bench, 1998, courtesy of RADI Designers
RADI Designers, Sleeping Cat Rug, 1999, courtesy of RADI Designers
RADI Designers, Ghost Miroir, 2001, courtesy of RADI Designers
RADI Designers, Abat Jour pour Bougie candleholder lamp, 1999, courtesy of RADI Designers
Jean-louis-André-Théodore Géricault, 1791-1824, A horse frightened by lighting, courtesy of the National Gallery
Salvador Dali, 1904-1989, courtesy of The Bridgeman Art Library, photo Roger Viollet, Paris

Karım Rashıd

Karim Rashid, Blobject Chair, 1999, courtesy of Karim Rashid
Archizoom Associati, Mies Chair, 1969, courtesy of Vitra Design Museum, © Vitra Design Museum, Weil am Rhein
Joe Columbo, Universale Chair No. 4867, 1965, courtesy of Vitra Design Museum, © Vitra Design Museum, Weil am Rhein
Gio Ponti, Superleggera Model No. 699, 1951-1957, courtesy of Vitra Design Museum, © Vitra Design Museum, Weil am Rhein
Gaetano Pesce, Pratt Chair, 1983, courtesy of Vitra Design Museum, © Vitra Design Museum, Weil am Rhein
Buckminster Fuller, Geodesic Dome, c. 1970, courtesy of the estate of R Buckminster Fuller
Michael Thonet, Chair Model No. 14, 1859, courtesy of Vitra Design Museum, © Vitra Design Museum, Weil am Rhein
Bang & OLufsen, Beomaster 1900, 1979
Karim Rashid, Time and Space, 2003, courtesy of Karim Rashid
Karim Rashid, PLOB interactive environment, 2001, courtesy of Karim Rashid
Karim Rashid, Crysalis and Butterfly, 2003, courtesy of Karim Rashid
Audi A2, 2003, courtesy of Simon Fox, Autocar magazine
Smart Car, 2003, courtesy of Simon Fox, Autocar magazine
Karim Rashid, Bloob Pedestal, 2004, courtesy of Karim Rashid
Karim Rashid, Fessura Mirror, 2004, courtesy of Karim Rashid
Karim Rashid, Picnic Bag, 2003, courtesy of Karim Rashid
Andy Warhol, 1928-1987, © The Guardian
Kevin Spacey © The Guardian
Damien Hirst © The Guardian

Tejo Remy

Tejo Remy, Bench of Balls, Museum Boijmans van Beuningen, Rotterdam, 2004, courtesy of Tejo Remy
Stiletto (Frank Schreiner), Consumer's Rest Chair, 1983, courtesy of Vitra Design Museum,
© Vitra Design Museum, Weil am Rhein
Ron Arad, Well Tempered Chair, 1986, courtesy of Ron Arad Studio
Tejo Remy, Installation, courtesy of Tejo Remy
Tejo Remy, Installation, courtesy of Tejo Remy
Oskar de Kiefte, The Converted Porsche 924, 1995, courtesy of Oskar de Kiefte
Tejo Remy, VROM Canteen, 2004, courtesy of Tejo Remy
Tejo Remy, Installation, courtesy of Tejo Remy
Oskar de Kiefte, Fiat Public, 1998, courtesy of Oskar de Kiefte

Arnout Visser

Arnout Visser, Real World Picture Reformer, 2001, courtesy of Arnout Visser

Michele de Lucchi, first chair, 1983, courtesy of Vitra Design Museum, © Vitra Design Museum, Weil am Rhein

Ingo Maurer, Birdie Chandelier, 2002, courtesy of Ingo Maurer

Foster and Partners, Hong Kong and Shanghai Banking Corp. HQ, Hong Kong, 1979-1986, courtesy of Foster and Partners, photo Ian Lambot

Garthamlock Water Towers, Glasgow, 2003, courtesy of Sharon Halliday, www.hiddenglasgow.com

Toilet, Edinburgh, 2004, © Paul Rodgers

Arnout Visser, Coca Cola Lamp, 2000, courtesy of Arnout Visser

Arnout Visser, Glasservies Centraal Museum, 1999, courtesy of Arnout Visser

Arnout Visser, Tegelkeuken, 2001, courtesy of Arnout Visser

Arnout Visser, Ice Cube Insulation Bowl, 2002, courtesy of Arnout Visser

Hummer H2 Sports Utility Vehicle, 2003, courtesy of Alex Milton, © Alex Milton

Adolf Hitler, 1889-1945, courtesy of The Bridgeman Art Library

Marcel Wanders

Marcel Wanders, Gobi Bath Tub, 2001, courtesy of Marcel Wanders Studio

Antonio Gaudi, La Sagrada Familia Interior, 1882-1926, courtesy of Ed Hollis, © Ed Hollis

Frank O Gehry, Cardboard Furniture, 1972, courtesy of Vitra AG, photo Hans Hansen

Philippe Starck, Louis XX Stacking Chair, 1992, courtesy of Vitra AG, photo Hans Hansen

Marcel Wanders, Knotted Chair, 1995, courtesy of Marcel Wanders Studio

Marcel Wanders, Coffee Table, 2004, courtesy of Marcel Wanders Studio

Marcel Wanders, Flare, 2003, courtesy of Marcel Wanders Studio

Le Corbusier, Notre Dame du Haut, Ronchamp, 1950-1954, courtesy of Jeffery Howe, © Jeffery Howe

Marcel Wanders, Fishnet Chair, 1995, courtesy of Marcel Wanders Studio

Marcel Wanders, Print, courtesy of Marcel Wanders Studio

Marcel Wanders, Egg Vase (Droog Design), 1997, courtesy of Marcel Wanders Studio

Marcel Wanders, Sponge Vase (Droog Design), 1997, courtesy of Marcel Wanders Studio

Marcel Wanders, Carbon Chair, 2004, courtesy of Marcel Wanders Studio

Porsche 928, c. 1988, courtesy of Ellie Gray, Porsche (UK), © Porsche AG

Pablo Picasso, 1881-1973, courtesy of The Bridgeman Art Library, photo Roger Viollet, Paris

Nelson Mandela © The Guardian

Tokujin Yoshioka

Tokujin Yoshioka, Honey-Pop Chair, 2001, courtesy of Tokujin Yoshioka

Jean Nouvel, L'Institut du Monde Arabe, 1987-1988, © Paul Rodgers

Gustav Eiffel, Eiffel Tower, 1889, © Paul Rodgers

Tokujin Yoshioka, MUJI Infill Renovation, 2003, courtesy of Tokujin Yoshioka

Tokujin Yoshioka, A-POC Shop Interior Design. 2001, courtesy of Tokujin Yoshioka

Tokujin Yoshioka, Hermes 'Air du temps' 2004, courtesy of Tokujin Yoshioka

Tokujin Yoshioka, Kiss me goodbye, 2004, courtesy of Tokujin Yoshioka

Audio Cassette Tape, 2004, © Paul Rodgers

The Enzo Ferrari, 2002, courtesy of Simon Fox, Autocar magazine

Tokujin Yoshioka, A-POC Making Issey Miyake and Dai Fujiwara Installation, 2001, courtesy of Tokujin Yoshioka

Tokujin Yoshioka, Wind of LED, 2004, courtesy of Tokujin Yoshioka

Tokujin Yoshioka, Nissan Showroom Concept Proposal, 2000, courtesy of Tokujin Yoshioka

Leonardo da Vinci, 1452-1519, courtesy of The Bridgeman Art Library

A

Albrecht, Donald, Lupton, Ellen and Skov Holt, Steven, 2000, *Design Culture Now*, Laurence King Publishing, London.

Albus, Volker, ed, 2000, *Icons of Design: The 20th Century*, Prestel Publishing, London.

Alessi, Alberto, 2001, *The Dream Factory: Alessi since 1921*, Electa, Milan.

Aexander, Christopher, 1964, *Notes on the Synthesis of Form*, Harvard University Press, MA.

Annink, Ed and Schwartz, Ineke, 2003, *Bright Minds, Beautiful Ideas: Bruno Munari, Charles and Ray Eames, Martí Guixé and Jurgen Bey*, Book Industry Services (BIS), Amsterdam.

Antonelli, Paola, ed, 2001, *Workspheres: Design and Contemporary Work Styles*, The Museum of Modern Art, New York.

Arad, Ron, Cappellini, Giulio, Guilfoyle, Ultan, Hodge, Brooke, Houseley, Laura, Maier-Aichen, Hansjerg, Niimi, Ryu, Ubeda, Ramón, White, Lisa and Ytterborn, Stefan, 2002, *Spoon*, Phaidon Press, London.

Asensio, Paco, 2002, *Product Design*, teNeues Publishing Group, New York.

B

Bang, Jens and Palshøj, Jørgen, 2000, *Bang & Olufsen: Vision and Legend*, Danish Design Centre, Copenhagen.

Bartolucci, Marisa and Cabra, Raul, 2004, *Compact Design Series: Karim Rashid*, Chronicle Books, San Francisco.

Basalla, George, 1988, *The Evolution of Technology*, Cambridge University Press, Cambridge.

Ber Tacchini, Giulia, Calcagni, Paola, Lazzara, Lucio Luzo and Rinetti, Riccardo, 2002, *The Official Point of View*, Enorme Film Arts, Milan.

Binet, Hélène, 1997, *A Passage Through Silence and Light*, Black Dog Publishing, London.

Boissière, Olivier, 1991, *STARCK®*, Taschen, Cologne.

Bonsiepe, Gui, 1999, *Interface An Approach to Design*, Jan van Eyck Akademie, Maastricht.

Bourdieu, Pierre, 1984, *Distinction: A Social Critique of the Judgement of Taste*, Harvard University Press, MA.

Bouroullec, Ronan and Bouroullec, Erwan, 2003, *Ronan and Erwan Bouroullec*, Phaidon Press, London.

Branzi, Andrea, 1987, *Domestic Animals: The Neoprimitive Style*, Thames and Hudson, London.

Bucciarelli, Louis L, 1994, *Designing Engineers*, The MIT Press, MA.

Busch, Akiko, 2002, *Design is...Words, Things, People, Buildings and Places*, Metropolis Books, Princeton Architectural Press, New York.

Byars, Mel, 1997, *50 Chairs: Innovations in Design and Materials*, RotoVision, Switzerland.

Byars, Mel, 1998, *50 Products: Innovations in Design and Materials*, RotoVision, Switzerland.

Byars, Mel, 1999, *100 Designs / 100 Years: Innovative Designs of the 20th Century*, RotoVision, Switzerland.

C

Cassagnau, Pascale and Pillet, Christophe, 1999, *Beef, Brétillot/Valette, Matali Crasset, Patrick Jouin, Jean-Marie Massaud: Starck's Kids?*, Éditions Dis Voir, Paris.

Castelli, Clino T, 1999, *Transitive Design: A Design Language for the Zeroes*, Electa, Milan.

Collings, Matthew, 2003, *Ron Arad*, Phaidon Press, London.

Cranz, Galen, 1998, *The Chair: Rethinking Culture, Body, and Design*, W W Norton and Company, New York.

Crompton, Dennis, ed, 1999, *Concerning Archigram...*, Archigram Archives, London.

Crozier, Ray, 1994, *Manufactured Pleasures: Psychological Responses to Design*, Manchester University Press, Manchester

D

Davey, Andrew, 2003, *Detail: Exceptional Japanese Product Design*, Laurence King Publishing, London.

Dawkins, Richard, 1989, *The Selfish Gene*, Oxford University Press, Oxford.

Dixon, Tom, 2000, *Rethink*, Conran Octopus, London.

Dormer, Peter, 1990, *The Meanings of Modern Design*, Thames and Hudson, London.

Dormer, Peter, 1993, *Design since 1945*, Thames and Hudson, London.

Droste, Magdalena, 1990, *bauhaus 1919-1933*, Taschen, Cologne.

Dyson, James, 1998, *Against the Odds: An Autobiography*, Orion Business Books, London.

Dytham, Mark and Klein, Astrid, 2002, *Klein Dytham Architecture: Tokyo Calling*, Birkhäuser, Basel.

F

Featherstone, Mike, 1991, *Consumer Culture and Postmodernism*, Sage Publications, London.

Fiell, Charlotte and Fiell, Peter, 1997, *1000 Chairs*, Taschen, Cologne.

Fiell, Charlotte and Fiell, Peter, 1999, *Design of the 20th Century*, Taschen, Cologne.

Fiell, Charlotte and Fiell, Peter, 2000, *Industrial Design A-Z*, Taschen, Cologne.

Fiell, Charlotte and Fiell, Peter, 2003, *Designing the 21st Century*, Taschen, Cologne.

Fiell, Charlotte and Fiell, Peter, 2003, *Industrial Design*, Taschen, Cologne.

Forty, Adrian, 1986, *Objects of Desire: Design and Society, 1750-1980*, Thames and Hudson, London.

Future Systems, eds., 1999, *More For Inspiration Only*, John Wiley and Sons, London.

G

Grosenick, Uta and Riemschneider, Burkhard, 2002, *Art Now: 137 Artists at the Rise of the New Millenium*, Taschen, Cologne.

Guidot, Raymond and Boissière, Olivier, 1997, *Ron Arad*, Éditions Dis Voir, Paris.

Guixé, Martí, 2002, *Martí Guixé: 1:1*, 010 Publishers, Rotterdam.

Guixé, Martí, 2003, *Libre de Contexte/Context-Free/Kontext-Frei*, Birkhäuser, Basel.

H

Hauffe, Thomas, 1998, *Design: A Concise History*, Laurence King Publishing, London.

Heskett, John, 1980, *Industrial Design*, Thames and Hudson, London.

van Hinte, Ed and Bakker, Conny, 1999, *Tresspassers*, 010 Publishers, Rotterdam.

Höcker, Christoph, 2000, *Architecture: A Concise History*, Laurence King Publishing, London.

I

Inflate, 1998, *Swell*, Verlag Form, Frankfurt am Main.

J

Jodidio, Philip, 1998, *Santiago Calatrava*, Taschen, Cologne.

Jones, John Chris, 1992, *Design Methods*, Van Nostrand Reinhold, New York.

Joris, Yvonne, 1999, *Wanders Wonders: Design for New Age*, 010 Publishers, Rotterdam.

Julier, Guy, 2000, *The Culture of Design*, Sage Publications, London.

K

Kenya, Hara, 2000, *Re Design: Daily Products of the 21st Century*, Takeo Co. Ltd., Tokyo.

Kaplicky, Jan, 1996, *Future Systems: For Inspiration Only*, John Wiley and Sons, London.

de Kiefte, Oskar, 2001, *40% Auto*, Centrum Beeldende Kunst, Utrecht.

Koolhaas, Rem and Mau, Bruce, 1995, *S,M,L,XL*, The Monacelli Press, New York.

Koolhaas, Rem, Boeri, Stefano, Kwinter, Sanford, Tazi, Nadi and Obrist, Hans Ulrich, 2001, *Mutations*, Actar, Barcelona.

Koolhaas, Rem, ed, 2002, *The Harvard Guide to Shopping*, Taschen, Cologne.

Koolhaas, Rem, 2004, *Content*, Taschen, Cologne.

L

Lawson, Brian, 1990, *How Designers Think*, Butterworth-Architecture, Oxford.

Lefteri, Christof, 2001, *Plastic (Materials)*, RotoVision, Switzerland.

Libeskind, Daniel, 1992, *Countersign*, Rizzoli International Publications, New York.

Lorenz, Christopher, 1986, *The Design Dimension: Product Strategy and the Challenge of Global Marketing*, Blackwell, Oxford.

Lucie-Smith, Edward, 1993, *Furniture: A Concise History*, Thames and Hudson, London.

M

Manzini, Ezio, 1986, *The Material of Invention*, Arcadia, Milan.

Millet, Joaquim Ruiz, 2003, *Martí Guixé-Food Design*, Galeria H2O, Barcelona.

Morrison, Jasper, 1998, *A World Without Words*, Lars Müller Publishers, Switzerland.

Munari, Bruno, 1994, *Munari's Machines*, Corraini Editore, Mantova.

Myerson, Jeremy, 2001, *IDEO: Masters of Innovation*, Laurence King Publishing, London.

N

Norman, Donald A, 1988, *The Psychology of Everyday Things*, Basic Books, New York.

O

Okada, Takahiko, ed, 1986, *Isamu Noguchi*, Chronicle Books, San Francisco.

P

Papanek, Victor, 1972, *Design for the Real World*, Thames and Hudson, London.

Pavitt, Jane, 2000, *Brand.new*, V&A Publications, London.

Payne, Alexander, ed, 1999, *We Like This! Michael Young*, Black Dog Publishing, London.

Payne, Alexander, ed, 1999, *Ideas=Book, Azumi*, Black Dog Publishing, London.

Payne, Alexander, ed, 2004, *I'll Keep Thinking, Nick Crosby*, Black Dog Publishing, London.

Pernodet, Philippe and Mehly, Bruce, 2000, *Luigi Colani*, Éditions Dis Voir, Paris.

Petroski, Henry, 1993, *The Evolution of Useful Things*, Pavilion Books Ltd., London.

Pevsner, Nikolaus, 1936, *Pioneers of the Modern Movement: From William Morris to Walter Gropius*, Harmondsworth, London.

Philippi, Simone, 2000, *STARCK*, Taschen, Cologne.

R

Ragheb, J. Fiona, ed., 2001, *Frank Gehry, Architect*, Guggenheim Museum Publications, New York.

Ramakers, Rene and Bakker, Gijs, eds., 1999, *Couleur Locale: DROOG Design for Oranienbaum*, 010 Publishers, Rotterdam.

Ramakers, Rene and Bakker, Gijs, eds., 1998, *DROOG Design: Spirit of the Nineties*, 010 Publishers, Rotterdam.

Rashid, Karim, 2002, *Karim Rashid: I Want to Change the World*, Rizzoli, New York.

Rawsthorn, Alice, 1999, *Marc Newson*, Booth-Clibborn Editions, London.

Raymond Loewy Foundation Intenational, ed, 2002, *St Moritz Design Summit*, Arnoldsche Art Publishers, Stuttgart.

Redhead, David, 2000, *Products of our Time*, Birkhäuser, Basel.

Redhead, David, 2001, *The Power of 10: Ten Products by Ten British product Designers*, Laurence King Publishing, London.

Redhead, David, 2001, *Industry of One: Designer-Makers in Britain 1981-2001*, Crafts Council, London.
Rowe, Peter G, 1987, *Design Thinking*, The MIT Press, MA.

S

Schiffer, Michael Brian, 1999, *The Material Life of Human Beings: Artifacts, Behavior and Communication*, Routledge, London.
Schneider, Bernhard, 1999, *Daniel Libeskind: Jewish Museum Berlin*, Prestel Verlag, Munich.
Schouwenberg, Louise and Jongerius, Hella, 2003, *Hella Jongerius*, Phaidon Press, London.
Skeens, Nick and Farrelly, Liz, 2000, *Future Present*, Booth-Clibborn Editions, London.
Smith, Paul, 2003, *You Can Find Inspiration in Everything-And If You Can't, Look Again*, Thames and Hudson, London.
Spector, Nancy, ed., 2002, *Matthew Barney: The Cremaster Cycle*, Guggenheim Museum Publications, New York.
Sudjic, Deyan, 1985, *Cult Objects: The Complete Guide to Having it All*, Paladin, London.
Sudjic, Deyan, 1999, *Ron Arad*, Laurence King Publishing, London.

T

Tambini, Michael, 1999, *The Look of the Century: Design Icons of the 20th Century*, Dorling Kindersley Publishing, London.
Teunissen, Jose and van Zijl, Ida, eds., 2000, *DROOG and Dutch Design, From Product to Fashion: The Collection of the Centraal Museum Utrecht*, Centraal Museum, Utrecht.
Thackara, John, 1988, *Design after Modernism: Beyond the Object*, Thames and Hudson, London.
Thackara, John, 1997, *Winners! How Today's Successful Companies Innovate by Design*, Gower, Aldershot.

U

Ulrich, Karl T and Eppinger, Steven D, 1995, *Product Design and Development*, McGraw-Hill, New York.
Vitra Design Museum, 1997, *Dimensions of Design—100 Classical Seats*, Vitra Design Museum, Weil am Rhein.
Votolato, Greg, 1998, *American Design in the Twentieth Century*, Manchester University Press, Manchester.

V

Vrontikis, Petrula, 2002, *Inspiration=Ideas: A Creativity Sourcebook for Graphic Designers*, Rockport Publishers Inc., MA.

W

Wake, Warren K and Kornhaber, Mindy L, 2000, *Design Paradigms: A Sourcebook for Creative Visualization*, John Wiley and Sons, New York.
Walker, John A, 1989, *Design History and the History of Design*, Pluto Press, London.
Whitely, Nigel, 1993, *Design for Society*, Reaktion Books, London.
Woodham, Jonathan, 1997, *Twentieth Century Design*, Oxford University Press, Oxford.

Y

Yelavich, Susan, 1997, *Design for Life*, Cooper-Hewitt National Design Museum and Rizzoli, New York.
Yoshioka, Tokujin, 2002, *Tokujin Design*, Gap Publication, Tokyo.
van Zijl, Ida, 1997, *Droog Design 1991–1996*, Centraal Museum, Utrecht.

Black Dog Publishing

Architecture Art Design Fashion History
Photography Theory and Things

Designed by Emilia Gómez López @ BDP

ISBN 1 904772 00 5

British Library cataloguing-in-publication data
A CIP record for this book is available from the British Library

Black Dog Publishing Limited
Unit 4.04
Tea Building
56 Shoreditch High Street
London E1 6JJ UK
tel: +44 (0) 20 7613 1922
fax: +44 (0) 20 7613 1944
email: info@bdpworld.com
www.bdpworld.com